780.23
POP

D1120363

THE BUSINESS OF GETTING MORE GIGS

By
Bob Popyk

7/4/12

7-30-07

QUALITY 10 KS.

MWL

The Business of
GETTING
MORE GIGS
AS A PROFESSIONAL MUSICIAN

BOB POPYK
Columnist for the *International Musician*

HAL·LEONARD®

Copyright © 2003 by Bob Popyk

All rights reserved. No part of this book may be reproduced or utilized in any form or by any means, electronic or mechanical, including photocopying, recording, or any other information storage retrieval system, without permission in writing from the Publisher, except by a reviewer, who may quote brief passages for review.

Published by Hal Leonard Corporation
7777 W. Bluemound Rd.
P.O. Box 13819
Milwaukee, WI 53213, USA

Trade Book Division Editorial Offices:
151 West 46th Street, 8th Floor
New York, NY 10036

Visit Hal Leonard online at www.halleonard.com

ISBN: 0-634-05842-8

Library of Congress Control Number: 2003106523

Printed in the United States of America
First Edition

10 9 8 7 6 5 4 3 2 1

"Bob's columns in the *International Musician* support the AFM's belief that musicians can't "go it alone." Today's professional musicians need support, ideas and help to maintain a decent wage. It's great to see so many ideas put together in one book. There is no "silver bullet" for getting more work. Not everything works for everybody, but one idea put to good use could increase casual dates for working musicians tremendously...and Bob has some great ideas."

Thomas Lee, *President, American Federation of Musicians of the United States and Canada*

"The International Musician is happy to have Bob Popyk as a regular monthly columnist. His articles are well read, and he generates extensive feedback from all types of professional musicians looking to keep their calendars full. The music business IS a business. This book has some great ideas to make that business easier."

Florence Nelson, *Secretary-Treasurer, American Federation of Musicians in the United States and Canada*

"Today you need more than talent to succeed. It's a shame that there are a lot of untalented musicians making serious money, while talented guys have difficulty getting playing dates. But it's a marketing business, and most of all, it is a BUSINESS. That coupled with talent can put you way ahead of everybody."

Vince Falcone, *Former conductor and pianist with Frank Sinatra, now working with Tony Bennett and Steve Lawrence & Eydie Gorme*

"I wish they taught marketing yourself as a professional musician along with learning to play. If more people new the possibilities of an exciting musical career, and how to go about it, there would be many more musicians getting more work and creating more revenue for themselves. Music stores wouldn't be able to stock enough instruments!"

Joe Lamond, *President, National Association of Music Merchants*

"If all aspiring musicians read this book, our instrument sales could increase just because of an expanded market for professional instruments from musicians making more money at their career!"

Dennis Houlihan, *President, Roland Corp. US*

Table of Contents

PREFACE

PREFACE

Talent Alone Does Not Always Equal Success

A talented musician is not always assured of a calendar full of well-paid playing dates, recording contracts, and residual revenue. But a talented musician with some business smarts, a marketing plan, good promotional material, plus some personality and initiative can reach heights other musicians never attain.

It doesn't matter what type of music you play, or what type of work you're going after. It could be club dates, weddings, corporate venues, shows, parties, recording contracts, or anything that pays well. Just because you play great doesn't mean your phone is going to ring with people looking to hire you, or booking agents are going to beat a path to your door. You have to make it happen.

There are a lot of different ideas in this book for taking your career to another level. It's a compilation of columns I've written for the *International Musician* over the years. Not everything is for everybody. Take the ideas you like, give them a shot, and you could very well find something that will bring in not only more work, but better paying work too.

It takes more than talent. There are a lot of out-of-work talented musicians. You need to add business savvy and marketing smarts, along with a good attitude. Then no one can stop you.

See you on the top of the charts, or on the way to the bank!

Bob Popyk

Chapter 1

ATTITUDE

ONE

Are You Proactive
or Reactive?

You are a musician. A professional. Your talent brings in revenue. It's how you make a living. There are only two ways to find gigs and to make money as a musician: 1) you can go out and find work, or 2) you can wait until work finds you.

If you are going to take the proactive approach by finding work and creating gigs for yourself, you need to be a little aggressive and assertive. And that means selling yourself. To some musicians, "selling" is a distasteful word. To others, it's a way to increase visibility and come up with creative ways to use your talent to bring in money. If you are the reactive type of musician who would rather wait for the phone to ring, that's your choice.

However, this book isn't about wasting your talent by waiting for the phone to ring. It's about ideas for finding casual work dates, creating job opportunities, and promoting yourself as a professional musician. Not all ideas are going to appeal to everyone. You can take the ones you like the best and give them a shot. If you don't like any, you have the right to sit back and do nothing. I guess it's a matter of how badly you want to work and what work you are willing to take.

The music business is not at all like it was in the past. But the world isn't like it used to be either. I remember my music teacher telling me, "When the parade passes, you have to march." Either you keep up, or you get left behind. If playing music is your livelihood, and if you rely on steady work to pay the bills, sometimes you just can't wait for those great, high-paying, "I won't play anything but this type of music" gigs to appear. You have to go out and find ways to earn a living using your music skills. It's better than having to say, "You want fries with that?" You have to make it happen, and in this day and age, sometimes you have to compromise and work less-rewarding jobs, keep on top of trends, promote yourself to the max, and work for years to become an overnight success.

If you're going to be proactive, you need to be professional. You need a Web presence. This means taking the time to learn some computer programs, or find someone to do it for you. (If you don't want to shell out big bucks for your own Web site, that 15-year-old kid next door can probably help you out.) You need e-mail, a digital answering machine or voice mail, a cell phone, and a fax machine. You need to be easily accessible at all times. You never know when someone is trying to reach you to book a gig or sign a new contract—don't miss out!

People who book bands and singles want more for less. It's a fact of life. They're looking for talented musicians who know a thing or two about technology. You need to learn about sequencers, pre-recorded soundtracks, MIDI, and how to take advantage of new sound modules. If you're going to book more gigs in the future, you have to stop living in the past. Find out what's hot and what's not. Check your image. Look as if you're successful, update your song list, and update your demo CD while you're at it.

I received a business card the other day from a young musician who plays professionally in Chicago, Illinois. It listed his Web site, e-mail address, home phone, cell phone number, and instruments played. There was no address. Doesn't matter. He's available 24/7 by e-mail or phone. Check your business card. (You do have one, don't you?) How much information do you have on it, and does it show you are easily accessible? Does it list a Web site where someone can go to find out a lot more about you? Does it have several phone numbers and an e-mail address?

You have to sell yourself. That doesn't mean taking the used-car-salesman approach, cutting prices and hustling gigs. It means having some business savvy, the initiative to find or create work for yourself, and the assertiveness to try different approaches to see what works for you.

Now, if you are the strictly reactive type who doesn't mind waiting for the phone to ring, and you have your choice of music gigs that are out there, you don't need any of this. One reader likened the music business today to a funeral service. I'd rather not mourn about what used to be and grieve about the lack of gigs today. The music industry is only what you make it. I still have a

Being pro-active is what keeps the phone ringing and your calendar always full.

mortgage payment coming up next month, a credit card bill, taxes, insurance premiums, and a weekly visit to the grocery store. The money has to come from somewhere, and that means finding work and making sure it keeps coming in.

Being proactive is what keeps the phone ringing and your calendar full. If you don't want to "sell yourself," then don't. Be reactive. Just don't admonish the musicians who are coming up with new ways to make a living with their talent and finding various venues to play. The parade is passing. Keep up or watch it go by. I don't criticize anyone for doing either. You can be a thermometer and tell how things are, or a rheostat and make things change. It's your choice.

Ready,
FIRE, Aim!

Wherever we are in our musical career, there always seems to come a time when we wish we were at the next level. More gigs. Better work. Higher pay. The problem is, sometimes we are not marketing people. We're musicians, not promotional experts, and we practice our craft to excel in what we do. But playing better doesn't always mean getting paid better. Playing better also does not mean the phone will always ring. If you're looking to better yourself, you need to do something right away.

Don't put yourself in the "poor me" category of "nobody wants to book me or pay me what I'm worth." Do something about it. Take some action, and start with self-promotion. If you don't shine your own light and continually work to make it brighter, you won't get noticed as quickly or as regularly as the musicians who toot their own horn. Don't worry about what will work and what won't. Try a lot of things. Get yourself into the spotlight. Here are a few tips to become your own PR agent.

> **Don't worry about what will work and what won't— try a lot of things.**

1) Promote yourself, your talent, and your success. A great mailing list is invaluable, both for regular mail and e-mail. You need to create a list of people to regularly update on your playing engagements, accomplishments, and CDs. Show them you're thinking about them by mailing notices of events they might want to attend, thank-you notes, holiday cards, and notes of congratulations. Staying in touch is a critical part of promoting yourself. Getting your name out there could give you the advantage when someone makes a split-second decision on whom to hire. And it's easier to ask for more money if the person writing the check knows something about you.

2) Tell everyone about your goals. When you make a commitment, or set your sights to a higher level, tell people. Desire is an amazing thing. Goals are more likely to become reality if you talk about them. Plus, getting feedback on your goals can help you proceed with them. If you want to work in Vegas, talk about it. If doing Broadway shows is your dream, tell everyone. If you want to make twice or three times what you're earning now, let people know you're going to be raising your fee. Some might tell you you're crazy, but others will support your goal and come up with ideas to help you achieve it. The main thing is that input from other sources can accelerate your career. Remember, don't hide your talents or your goals under a bushel. Let people know about them.

3) Discover your uniqueness. You will get more work—or at least get paid more—if you are first, best, or different. If you are first with a unique sound, the best keyboard player in the area, or specialize in a music niche where fewer musicians are competing, you will probably command more visibility as well as more money. We can't be everything to everybody and expect to create a stir in the marketplace. If you are a rocker and are up against fierce competition in your area, maybe it's time to change your music venue if better gigs and more money are the most important things to you. However, if you truly dislike many kinds of music, chances are you are limited in what you can achieve. The best polka band in the state will make far more than any also-ran club act. The best Latin group in the area will usually pull in more than an average wedding band. And a great keyboard/single/ vocalist will get more gigs and make more money than a piano player with a big band. Get yourself out of any rut you might be in. Remember, the only difference between a grave and a rut is the

length, the depth, and the amount of time you're in it. It's your decision. How strong is your desire to accelerate your career?

4) Never bad-mouth other musicians. So what if they can't play their way out of a fake book? You never know when you might need them, or their good opinion of you. Watch it.

5) Keep your negative thoughts to yourself. If you start saying the music business stinks; nobody appreciates talent; the DJs are getting all the wedding work; club owners are demented, inhuman, greedy parasites; and you can't get a recording gig to save your fanny, you will fulfill your own prophecy. Remember, whether you think you can or you think you can't, you're absolutely right.

Here's the kicker: don't worry about the results of what you're doing to promote yourself. It's not ready, aim, fire. You can think too much, and all of a sudden you start saying, "If only I had a better instrument," or "If I only lived in New York or Nashville," or "If only I could get a break." Forget it. Change your thinking to ready, FIRE, aim! Just do something right away. Which, of course, is a lot better than doing nothing, like most musicians who are unhappy with their careers. The world does not owe you a living. You make your own success. Fire when ready!

ou Let Your Professional de Show Through?

READY, FIRE, AIM!

...fines a professional as "one who is engaged in a ...ation that requires advanced education or training," or "someone who follows an occupation as a means of livelihood or for gain, in a distinguished manner as to separate themselves from an amateur."

You're a professional musician. To separate yourself from amateurs, your professionalism should always come through. When it doesn't, its absence casts a shadow on you, and sometimes on other musicians. Unprofessional behavior can take the form of bickering on stage, chastising other musicians in front of an audience, complaining, or just not giving your best. Unprofessional conduct comes in assorted sizes and degrees.

Here's a case in point. I was visiting one of my friends who owns a major company on the East Coast. He told me that they were having their annual meeting in a few months, and thought a trio with maybe a vocalist would be a nice touch. We checked around and found a band playing at a local nightspot. We went into the lounge area and sat at the bar. The weather outside was horrible, and there weren't a whole lot of people there. In fact, there were nine people including the bartender. I said to my friend, "I heard this group was one of the best, particularly the keyboard player who is outstanding. And the singer has a couple of CDs that were written up in several music magazines."

It came time for them to start, except they didn't start. The keyboard player spent a lot of time fiddling with the digital programming, and the singer complained about the lack of customers, the bad weather, and the fact that there was a silent TV still on. When they finally kicked off with a couple of tunes, the singer decided she didn't like the key and wanted a different tempo as well. The keyboard player couldn't get the sound he wanted and kept changing tones and background while he played. The drummer verbally expressed his displeasure at having to play for a handful of people on a snowy night, and the singer started audibly chatting with him about problems with her boyfriend.

> "I don't care how good they are— I hate their attitude."

After three tunes, she decided to sit down and have dinner. My friend suggested we leave, since he would never hire these people. As he put it, "I don't care how good they are, I hate their attitude." So we went someplace else. He just wanted to hear something "a little more professional."

The next place had a duo whose musical skills were only good; on a scale of 1 to 10 they would probably be about a 6. This bar had even fewer people. The difference was this little group played like they were in front of a full house, chatted with the few people at the bar, took requests, and acted as if they were having a good time. The customers were buying drinks (which made the bar owner happy), and my friend hired them for his company function. He said he wanted a "professional group." To him musical skill was secondary to attitude. Often the term "professional" is in the eye of the beholder.

I used to hire a drummer who was always late for gigs. He was definitely not professional. He was a great drummer with limited success. As Woody Allen said, "Ninety percent of success is just showing up." I replaced him with a drummer not quite as good, but someone I could count on, and the jobs kept coming in. Do you make it to your gigs on time? Do you treat your career as a living, or just a hobby that pays? Check your attitude. If you act like a professional, potential employers will know the difference.

Professionalism shows in your appearance, your music, your PR materials, your attitude, and your business skills. It's more than how well you play. It's being a well-rounded musician with a good attitude, personality, business skills, and a sense of what it takes to get ahead in the music business. You need to work on every aspect to keep your calendar full.

Fear of Rejection
Can Be Fear of Success

Rejection is a fact of life in the music business. Musicians contact clubs and corporate event people who reject them. Bands offer their services to people planning weddings, parties, and casual dates who reject them. Songwriters pitch songs to publishers who reject them. It's a virtual food chain of rejection. People think of musicians as products, not artists trying to make a living. You need to be able to deal with rejection on a regular basis to achieve any degree of success.

It's much easier to fail than to succeed. Fear of success can bring us down in a heartbeat. It can keep us from achieving our potential. The fear of success results from having a preconceived notion that it is incredibly hard to succeed. And fear of rejection supports it to the point that when you fail, you say to yourself, "I knew it all along." You start to think things are bad and they're going to get worse. No use trying to reach the next level; it's tough enough where you are right now. Why bother to go for those big-paying gigs, where you'll have to hear the word "no" more often? Why talk to everybody you know to get your name out, just to advance one more step toward rejection? I'll tell you why: because you just never know. Success could be the next person you talk to. I'll give you an example.

> **You need to be able to deal with rejection on a regular basis.**

Recently, I spoke at the National Association of Music Merchants convention in Nashville, Tennessee. This NAMM show was held in July at the Convention Center. It was a great gig for me because I love being in Music City and I like to look at the new instruments and talk to people in the music business. My talk was addressed to music store owners about "How to Increase Your Business by 25%... Starting Next Week!" One night after the show closed, I was sitting at the bar talking to some of my friends who were seated to my left. To the right of me was someone who seemed to be by himself.

When there was a lull in my conversation, he turned to me and said, "Are you with the convention?" I told him I was, and he asked what I did. I told him I was doing a program at the show on sales strategies. He asked if I had any connections in the song-writing end of the business. I said, "No." That didn't even faze him. Next thing I know he tells me he's a guitar player/song-writer, drives a cab part-time, and wants to know if I'd like to see any of his songs. Since he was a fellow union musician, I told him I'd take a look.

He pulled out a manila envelope with about a dozen songs. He then took out the first one and told me how he came to write it. He told me where his inspiration came from. He even sang a bit to show me how the melody went. My friends on the left started to look at him a little suspiciously, like maybe he had a couple of cocktails too many. I then told him it seemed like a great tune, but I wasn't in that part of the music business. Then he said to me, "I don't care. If I show these songs to enough people, somebody might like them and they might know someone who can help me get them published. I just have to talk to enough people. I can handle rejection, and I can handle success even better." Then he put his songs away and disappeared into the crowd.

I didn't think too much about it until yesterday, when I heard one of his tunes by a country artist on the radio. He must have showed them to people until he finally heard "yes." It only took him years of talking to a lot of people to be an overnight success. I don't remember his name. I only remember his tenacity, his drive, his personality, and his ambition.

Could you do it? Would you do it? Do you fear success so much that you let rejection get in your way? If you are satisfied in your own comfort zone, that's one thing. But if you want to expand your horizons and get a little higher on the success ladder, you will have a lot of people trying to kick your behind. And the higher up you go, the more your behind is exposed and apt to be kicked. Deal with it. Learn to handle it. All those noes can someday turn into one giant YES.

Visualize your success. Start to eliminate the negative influences in your life. Find and create reasons to feel good about yourself. Above all, accept the fact that rejection is something that's going to be there, and realize that success could be just a little ways down the road. In fact, it might be closer than you think.

How Badly Do You
Want to Work as a
Professional Musician?

Darrel has been a professional musician for about twenty-five years, and has never done anything else. He told me that things were bad in his town. Musicians were being replaced by DJs, clubs weren't using live music anymore, and corporate work dried up after the terrorist attack. There just wasn't enough going on to pay the bills as a musician.

Now, don't get me wrong, this guy is a terrific talent. Other keyboard players are in awe of how great this guy can play. His last job was five weeks ago. He called me to tell me about his plight and what I thought he should do. I gave him ten ideas:

1) Move to a bigger town.

2) Teach.

3) Find a church gig.

4) Work as a single on a cruise ship.

5) Look for jingle work with some ad agencies.

6) Contact local retail keyboard stores and offer your services for concerts and promotions (maybe at scale plus a percentage of instruments sold).

7) Find a backer for a CD and promote it yourself. Do your own PR to get airtime that could result in more visibility and better-paying gigs.

8) Investigate various charity functions and fundraisers within a fifty-mile radius. Let a sponsor know you can play for the cocktail party or any other part of the venue where music would be appropriate.

9) Come up with a program about music through the years, and do high school assembly programs around the state.

10) Look into corporate events coming to town, find out who the planners are, and suggest how you could add to the event.

When I gave him these suggestions, he said he didn't want to move because he had roots in his small town and liked living there. He hated teaching, even though he could make $60 an hour or more, because he didn't like the regimentation. Playing a church gig wasn't his thing, no matter how well it paid. He thought he would get seasick on a cruise ship. Jingle work didn't pay enough, and there was too much competition. He hated the thought of promoting instruments and doing concerts in a music store, and didn't want to impose on any of his "well-off" friends to back a CD. He didn't like the idea of finding a local sponsor for charity work, high school assembly programs are a drag, and getting any kind of corporate gig takes a lot of work. He'd rather wait for the phone to ring. And the phone just hasn't been ringing lately.

Investigate various charity functions and fundraisers within a fifty-mile radius.

I told him it was over. Find something else to do. He truly believes there is no work out there, his attitude is in the pits, and he tells everybody how cruel the world is to musicians. He has become a prophet of his own destiny. It's sad.

On the other side of the coin, I received a phone call from a professional trumpet player in the northeast. He said he works all the time and agreed about not "lowering himself" to get out there and play for free. He said there are a lot of gigs if you just exert yourself a little.

For example, he told me how he introduced himself to all the funeral directors in both areas where he belongs to the local union. When a veteran dies, the funeral director suggests to the family that taps be played at the gravesite. The funeral director acts as his agent. The musician gets paid the price of a four-hour gig, even though he only works a few minutes. I asked him what makes him unique at this. He said he hides out of sight and plays taps twice—once towards the grave, then he turns around and plays it the other way like an echo. He also has a pamphlet that tells about his service. A little morbid, maybe, but he does this every week. Sometimes several times a week. He says he has no competition; no one else wants to do it.

He told me he learned to play keyboard, so he can play trumpet with one hand and keyboard with the other. Corporate venues love him because they think it's unique. If it's an AFL-CIO-affili-

If you want to do something bad enough, you can always find a way to do it.

ated company, he makes sure they know he's a union musician. He does a lot of their cocktail parties and gets repeat work. He sings, too, and he sometimes emcees a function. He says it takes a lot of time staying in touch with the meeting planners, plus they change all the time. But he always asks for referrals, calls them on the phone, sends them thank-you notes, keeps them on his mailing lists, and sends them a gift at Christmas. He also has a bit where he does high school assembly programs talking about how music can enrich your life. He plays two trumpets at one time and the message is, "If you want to do something bad enough, you can always find a way to do it."

Now here's the kicker: he's not one of the top players in town, yet he works all the time. He has business sense, marketing smarts, and personality. He never cuts his price, and he never just sits around waiting for the phone to ring for his next gig. He's always finding different ways to earn a living as a professional musician.

So, if your calendar is not as full as you'd like, and the bucks aren't coming in as fast as you want, ask yourself, "How badly do I want to work?" Enough to be a little creative, somewhat assertive, and willing to go the extra mile? And do a little attitude check. See if you're in a rut. Thinking a little outside the box could result in some interesting work as a professional musician.

Ten Things to Remember
When Subbing on a Gig

Bill Evans, editor of *Gig* magazine, and I were discussing the pros and cons of taking a gig at the last minute with a group you hadn't worked with before, just because they were desperate for a musician to fill in. Some of these dos and don'ts were in an article in *Gig*, written by Brice Wightman, and I thought they really hit home.

You might be thinking that any paying gig is hard to turn down. But to really further your career, here are some things you might want to think about when someone calls and asks if you can play with them that night or that week because they are in a bind.

1) First of all, be honest. Be up front about your musical skills and the type of music you're being asked to play. If you know the material and are comfortable with it, it's a no-brainer. There's no reason not to take it. If the gig is a music style you are not familiar or comfortable with, and the leader wants you anyway, then you can still give it a shot, but be careful. The worst thing you can do is tell the leader you know all his stuff, and then get to the gig only to look like an amateur trying to play the music or read the charts. Sure, it's good to play many styles of music, but if you're a rock drummer who gets a call for a Latin gig and you think clave is a new item at Taco Bell, then pass.

Be up front about your musical skills.

2) When you get blind calls from leaders you don't know, ask where they got your name. This can give you a better idea of what caliber player they might be looking for. Ask some questions. Maybe it's a gig with musicians you are eager to work with, or

can learn something from. But think carefully about it if the musicians are way out of your league. You want repeat work, not a bad reputation for not being able to keep up.

3) Remember the phrase, "Show me the money"? Get the payment terms and hours in advance. If you're not familiar with the person who's hiring you, make sure there's no question of payment at the end of the night. You might want to ask them to send you an e-mail confirming your agreement, just so you have something to fall back on in case they start to get funny with money. Perhaps ask about their union status, and whether the job will be filed with the local union.

Leave your attitude at home...then, play your best.

4) When you take the gig, arrive early enough to set up your equipment and warm up. Leave your attitude at home. Make sure your axe is in shape and bring whatever gear you need. Double-check the small things like sticks, reeds, mouthpieces, strings, extension cords, or any accessories for whatever instrument you play. Then play your best.

5) Stay on your toes. Keep your eyes and ears wide open. This gig could be a great educational experience to improve your playing. Focus is the key. You want the other musicians to respect your playing ability and music smarts so you can get more calls to sub.

6) Don't try to be the star. Play what's required, but don't be a show-off. Blend with the group. You will get a lot more calls this way.

7) Network with the group. Hand out your card at the end of

the gig to the other musicians. Get the phone numbers and e-mail addresses of the other people in the group as well. Thank the leader for using you.

8) No drugs. No booze. Don't be an idiot. A bad reputation of this kind can kill any repeat work.

9) Know when to say no. Use your head. Know when to turn down a gig: if the job pays under scale, if it's too far to drive for too little money, if the group has had problems.

10) Remember, you're a professional, but many times you are only as good as your last gig. You build or start to destroy your reputation at every gig you play. Ask yourself if the subbing gig is going to enhance your career, keep it level, or start to bring it down. Then make your decision accordingly.

If you get good at filling in at the last minute, you'll get a reputation for being available, dependable, and the type of musician who can adapt easily. Your name will get around quickly. Keep in touch with all the local groups.

There will be times when someone really desperate calls you; it's only a few hours before the gig, and there is no one left to call. You're the only answer, and you can make the gig. So before you jump at the chance, use your head a little. Be honest about your talent, get straight on the money, and give it your best shot. You never know when that next sub job could be the start of something big.

Playing Well Does Not Always Mean a Full Calendar

I know a local keyboard player who is an incredible musician. He's not just good; he's great. He's probably one of the best keyboard players in the country. Well-known musicians seek him out when coming through his town hoping he will be playing somewhere they can hear him. He has the best state-of-the-art equipment. He sings well. He knows cover tunes better than the original artists. He has thousands of songs in his brain. He can play them in any key and can fit in with any group. As a single, he can compete with the best tight-knit group. Even with all these credentials and considering that he lives in a busy music town, my friend is lucky to play two nights a week. You see, in spite of his incredible musical ability, his attitude stinks. He hates requests. He is not a good people person. If his marketing skills are zero, his professionalism is negative ten.

The moral of the story? Talent alone does not automatically result in consistent, well-paying gigs. Just playing well does not always guarantee a full calendar of decent bookings.

If you are a little lacking in the personality-skills department, you probably won't create a rush of repeat business. Nobody likes to book a musician who is a pain. If you're doing a single, and customers "put bread in your jar and say, 'Man, what are you doing here?'" and your reply is, "This sucks, I wish I could play my own stuff," chances are you won't be playing Carnegie Hall or working with Shania Twain anytime soon. Playing what customers want may not excite the heck out of you, but remember—a bad day at a well-paying gig sure beats a good day flipping burgers at McDonald's.

Nobody likes to book a musician who is a pain.

You don't have to be a marketing genius to get well-paying gigs, either. But you need at least the basics. You need a reliable answering machine and a reputation for returning calls. Simple things like keeping a master calendar so you never miss a gig or get there late are important. You need business cards with current phone numbers, some promotional print pieces on yourself, and some decent business chops. This is only, of course, if you really want to succeed. Some musicians don't care one way or the other. Then they wonder why someone else "gets all the breaks."

To achieve real success, you have to make your own breaks. This might mean some serious soul-searching about what type of music you like to play versus the type of music that people are willing to pay to hear. It also might mean doing some out-of-the-way things that will make you look a lot better than you may be. Here's a good example.

There's a club in the northeast that pays more than scale and constantly rotates bands. A typical Saturday night will have the band play from 10 p.m. until 2 a.m. The average band will arrive at 9 p.m. and schlep the gear in. They tune and do sound checks from 9:30 until 10. They annoy the heck out of patrons with constant "Check … check … one… two… check… check." Feedback comes from the amps. A cymbal stand tips over and startles a couple walking in. The band then starts at about 10:05, maybe later. The first thing that comes out of their mouths is, "Hey! How's everybody doing?" And nobody responds because nobody cares.

Compare this with the group who sets up during the afternoon, then makes an entrance (rather than just stumbling on stage) at 10:00 sharp. A fog machine kicks off the show, and the band starts a cassette that announces: "Ladies and gentlemen, the Flamingo Club proudly presents Music Inc. recording artists, Your Band!" (So what if it's their own label? The audience doesn't need to know.) And then they walk on stage and immediately start to play. The crowd thinks the band is somebody special, the musicians feel like they're somebody special, and the club owner rebooks them for four more dates before they're through their second set. It's show business. No, actually it's the entertainment business. Business is the key word.

Talent alone won't ensure repeat gigs. Catering to the crowd, not ticking off the club owner, tweaking your personality, and using some creative business smarts will. Talent alone won't always bring in the big bucks or stardom. Talent + personality + business smarts + attitude + a little luck = success.

Ego Satisfaction
Can Equal Starvation

If there is anything professional musicians learn over time, it's that playing music just to feed personal satisfaction can get in the way of making decent money. You know how it goes. A band has been playing cover tunes for years and starts making an above-average amount of money. Audiences love them, and they get tons of work. During practice one week, somebody scribbles down lyrics that could be just as good as any of the old hits, maybe even better musically. Everyone plays around with it for a while, and the decision is made to perform this original work at the next gig. The band loves the song and starts to get really excited.

The band works on more original songs. Their songs rock, but the crowd wants tunes they can recognize. Soon the cover songs start to be a drag. The band no longer plays them with the same intensity. They start to talk about only taking gigs where they can play mostly their own material. They think that artistically and creatively it's the only way to go. Heck, who knows great music better than great musicians? Unfortunately it becomes a career disaster for the band. The gigs dry up. The musicians take part-time jobs. The band finally breaks up, and the musicians go their separate ways playing gigs with other cover bands.

Ego gets in the way. Ego can be a career killer to a budding musician or aspiring band.

Singles can suffer the same syndrome. A lounge piano player who just hates songs from a certain recording artist starts to lecture patrons on their musical taste, and when someone requests one of the artist's songs, he just doesn't want to play it. The next week he's looking for work at another club and doesn't know why the last place didn't keep him on. The moral here is that being a great musician doesn't always keep a gig. If you're doing casual dates, club dates, or corporate gigs, just playing your best doesn't mean you're going to make it. If you're there to entertain, you have to entertain. That's the kicker. We're entertainers as well as musicians. If we're really going to get the gigs that pay the bigger bucks, we've got to check our egos at the door.

Unfortunately, learning to play better is not always the answer to keeping a gig—or finding better gigs. Tweaking your personality, however, can sometimes pay big dividends. Being a creative genius musically doesn't always mean success. People have to like you and what you play. Here's a suggestion: go to your local library and get a book on marketing or personality skills, maybe a Dale Carnegie book.

If we're really going to get the gigs that pay the bigger bucks, we've got to check our egos at the door.

Check out the groups or singles working clubs where you'd like to work. Can you do a better job music-wise? But more important, can you do a better job entertainment-wise? Are you a crowd pleaser, or are you an ego pleaser? Tough question. Being a crowd pleaser is a job. Feeding your own ego becomes a hobby. The problem is that hobbies don't pay well. We have to remind ourselves once in a while that we play music for a living. We are WORKing musicians. Playing a lousy gig can be better than many other jobs that pay far less.

If the type of music you're playing right now is working, if it's bringing in decent revenue, and the only person who doesn't like it is you, you may find yourself on a downward spiral if you start to change it. You might have to grin and bear it—if it's not broke, think very carefully before you try to fix it. Don't let a DJ grab a gig from you because he or she reaches into the case and spins what the audience wants to hear, smiles all the time, warms up to the audience, and never complains. You have talent, you can do it live, and you're better. Aren't you?

There's an old saying in the sales business: the easiest way to close a sale is to find out what the customer wants and give it to him. That works for the music business too. If the people who are paying you want to hear something you think is musically inferior, suck it up and do it. And do it well. You're only as good as your last gig. Ego can ruin a great musical career.

Original Tunes
and Survival

I guess I struck a nerve when I wrote that I thought playing more of what the audience wants to hear (cover tunes, requests) could generate more work than playing just the stuff a musician likes (original tunes). (See "Ego Satisfaction Can Equal Starvation.") Many of the letters I got raised some excellent points for consideration. I like to keep an open mind, and I am happy to listen to constructive criticism.

One musician asserted that "creativity is not necessarily ego ... I feel that inspiration comes from a place other than the ego." He also made a point when he said that "in order to make it big, a musician absolutely has to find some original voice."

Another musician had some excellent ideas. He hit a couple of things right on: "Original tunes, I find, can be introduced on gigs if the writer/player thinks ahead. Play one original a set and give it a little intro—'Here's a song I think could be a hit like the last tune I played.'" He added, "If they want 'As Time Goes By,' give it to them, but don't crush your own hopes of writing your own classic. 'As Time Goes By' was once an original that a hopeful songwriter warbled while thinking nervously, 'Who will ever want to hear this?'"

Many creative musicians deal with an inherent conflict of art versus income.

I thought they had some good points I hadn't originally considered. The majority of the other letters I received had really good ideas, but I think a few may have missed the point—especially where revenue wasn't an issue. Some musicians don't work just for the money, and that's their call. I respect their choice. But I also realize that there can be a fine line on how to handle original tunes and still make the bucks while satisfying an audience. Anything in moderation can be okay, as long as it doesn't start to irritate the audience, or generally not fit in with the gig you're performing. Also, personality plays a huge part. Working the crowd is the other secret. The problem escalates if attitude sets in. We get paid to give people what they want. And we work better if it's what we want, as well. It's nice when both happen.

Perhaps this musician put it most succinctly when he wrote, "Many creative musicians deal with an inherent conflict of art versus income...that's part of the very nature of what we choose to do."

Attitude Makes
a Difference

I've played a lot of gigs over the years with a drummer who works very steadily. We both come from a small town in upstate New York with a population of about 29,000 people. He's still there. I left to do other things along with being a musician, but he was content living in a small town and just wanted to play drums. I never remember him being without work and I don't remember him having another job. He played drums and taught for a living. When we were young we went to the same high school and played any kind of gig that would pay us. We joined the union at the same time and remained members. Being a musician is the only thing he wanted. It is the only thing he knows. With me it's more of a hobby now; to him it's his profession.

A few months ago he was diagnosed with throat cancer, and his friends held a benefit for him to help with what his insurance wouldn't cover. I couldn't believe the turnout. Musicians from all over the state showed up. It was really cool. He was too sick to be there himself, but his wife and kids came for him. I got to talk with some musicians I hadn't seen in years. I asked them why Dick got so much work in a town that was continually losing population, that had to merge with a bigger local, that has not much of a live music scene, and whose biggest employer is a state prison.

The best insight came from a guitarist who has played with Dick for years. I asked how he got continuous work. He never had his own band, he was always a sideman. Was it because he was an outstanding musician? Was it because he was a good networker? The answers were surprisingly simple.

1) He was dependable. You could always count on him being there.

2) He always showed up on time.

3) He never had an attitude. He always smiled and got along with everybody. He was fun to be with.

4) He played his best no matter the type of music or venue.

5) He was a good musician. Maybe not great, but he was good and he could read.

How many gigs have you played where one of the musicians came late, or worse yet, didn't show up at all? Have you played with musicians who have constant excuses for being late, like, "My car had a flat," "I thought it started later," and so on? Dependability starts with showing up for the gig on time. Excuses don't cut it. The reality is, being late means you simply didn't leave enough time to deal with any problem that might arise.

Dependability starts with showing up for your gigs on time.

You limit your work by being too selective about what music you want to play. If you can't stand the venue, don't take the gig. Don't whine if you don't like the kind of music you're asked to play. Of course, you might have to expand your horizons and work on your attitude if you want more work than you're getting right now. It's a decision you have to make.

Also, if your chops aren't good enough to work with the best, maybe you should do something to take your talent up a notch. Your music is your craft, and you continually have to put yourself in a learning mode. That means constantly working on your reading skills so you can play anything put in front of you. While you're green you're growing, when you're ripe you rot. Your teacher was right—continue to practice. Work at your craft. Do a little soul-searching about the traits listed. How do you compare? Do you fall short in any category? How could you improve? And how's your attitude when out on a gig? Do you show up on time, go along with the program, and give 110 percent?

As musicians, our lives are not structured, and we often take advantage of a less than regimented routine. Don't be lazy. Maybe you are not punching a clock, but that next gig is a job that could lead to other gigs. Attitude really does make a difference.

Eight Simple Ways to Get Repeat Club Bookings

I know a country artist who's with a band that plays in some of the major clubs in his part of the country. They get a lot of work, and get booked at some clubs on a regular basis. We were talking the other day about how his band gets repeat work, what club owners look for in a band, and how they decide who makes a return trip. He says that while musical talent is important, there are other things club owners take into consideration. As he puts it, "Their business is not to manage bands; their business is running the club." Here's his advice on how you can get more repeat gigs.

1) Arrive early at the club. Allow yourself enough time so that after you set up, you will still have a half hour or so before the first set. This gives you a chance to get your head together and focus on your set list and the venue itself. Also, this gives you a little leeway for traffic, flat tires, and weather. Club owners have heard all the excuses in the world for why the group or one of the musicians showed up late. Forget the excuses. Plan to get there way ahead of time.

2) Always be nice to the waiters, waitresses, and bartenders. Even though you're an employee as well, make sure you tip them and treat them nicely. If they're on your side, they can make life a whole lot easier for you. In some cases, their opinions can influence whether you're hired again or not. Be respectful to the other workers.

3) Go easy on the drinking. Contrary to popular misconception, alcohol does not make you play better. This doesn't mean you have to act like you're at an AA meeting. Moderation is the

key. And, as my friend puts it, "I won't work with any musician who has anything to do with drugs." No drugs. Period.

4) Make sure that at least your front person talks to the audience during the set. Develop some rapport, and whatever you do, don't be standoffish. Don't let your ego get out of control. Don't insult anyone in the room, no matter how far-out their request may seem, or how obnoxious they may act. Schmooze. Get your audience to relate to you and your group. A little interaction can produce great chemistry and really encourage audience support.

5) This is important: never lose your temper. Get along with your fellow musicians, your sound people, and your set-up crew. Even if there are disputes between your band members, never let them affect the onstage performance. It only reflects poorly on you and is incredibly unprofessional. You want an image of unity. Leave your problems in the rehearsal room, in the truck, or at home. Don't bring them to the club.

Remember that the club's business is ringing the register.

6) Remember that the club's business is ringing the register, not annoying customers. Check the sound system, the amps, and the microphones hours before the gig when there are only a few people in the room. Make sure the system is squared away well before you start the first set.

7) Check with the club owners at the end of the night or the next day to make sure things went well. Ask for any input they might have. Let them know you have their best interests at heart. You want to make sure the owner was happy, and if it's the last night, make it clear you'd like to come back. In other words, don't

complain about the house, the crowd, or the setup if you want repeat work.

8) Don't wait to be asked—follow up. Contact the club owner a week or so after your show and actually ask for another booking. Say what a good time you had, how well the audience responded, and how you can't wait to play the venue again. Hey, if you don't ask, you don't get.

Okay, maybe that's too simple. But, as this musician says, "If it's so simple, why don't all bands do it?" Do a little soul-searching. How do you stack up? It has nothing to do with song lists or anything regarding talent. It's attitude, personality, schmoozing skills, and a little common sense. These business smarts can make your club date go a lot smoother—with a minimum of stress and a maximum of fun as well.

Success May Be Hiding
Just Around the Corner

We all have bad days. Sometimes bad weeks. Maybe the gigs aren't coming in as fast as you would like. Maybe your calendar is full, but the gigs stink. Maybe you feel your career should be at a higher level, but you're still stuck playing for scale at a place that just doesn't appreciate you. C'mon, lighten up. You could be serving Slurpees at the 7-Eleven. Success or a decent break could just be a couple of choruses away.

Just when you think you're stuck in a rut, and you're serving a sentence of Saturday afternoon weddings and scale work at one of the local saloons, things can change. You never know who's going to hear you and help take you or your group to a higher level. That's why you always have to be at the top of your game if you have any aspirations of moving up. Don't make the mistake of playing less than your best just because the gig isn't exactly your dream gig...even if it's the downright pits.

You never know who's going to hear you and help take you to a higher level.

Lou Holtz is one of the most famous football coaches in North America. He is the former coach of Notre Dame, and probably one of the finer motivators of all time. Lou likes to say, "Difficulty and adversity are good for you. They make you stronger; they help you grow." That's not only true in football, it's true in the music business as well.

The biggest problem, though, is that in the music business, we start to become prophets of our own destiny. How many times have the following negative words and phrases come out of your mouth or the mouth of a member of your band?

1) "Nobody wants to hire live music anymore."
2) "You can't make a living playing music in this town."
3) "We're lucky to get scale."
4) "I hate playing this crap."
5) "Nobody wants to hear good music anymore."
6) "Clubs can't pay musicians what they're worth."
7) "This is a weekend town—musicians can't make a living here."

If you believe it, then it must be so. Therefore, if this is starting to sound familiar, you have two options:quit, or do something about it.

If quitting is the road you choose to travel, that's your prerogative. If you'd rather do something about it, then forget the self-pity, the negativity, and the whining. Get yourself a better press kit, an up-to-date demo video, and a quality promotional package. Start using the phone for a little outbound telemarketing. Ask for referrals. Ask yourself, "How badly do I want more work, or better work? What am I willing to give up for it?" Nothing good comes easily. Are you willing to play more cover songs even if you like just doing originals? Are you willing to travel a little more or even move if it's necessary? Have you checked the AFM list of agents in your area to perhaps get better representation? Are you networking with other musicians? Have you cut a recent CD that showcases your best talents? Do you have a separate brochure just for corporate work? Have you made friends with the media? Do the people who work at your local radio stations know you, mention you once in a while, or even play your stuff? Do you add to your mailing list regularly? Do you even have a mailing list, both regular mail and e-mail?

What can you do this week to get more work or better work next week? Do a little soul-searching. Are you doing charity work so you can get more exposure and be a public service to your community as well? Are you getting PR in your local paper on a regular basis? Are your chops as good as they could be? Do you run circles around most of the other musicians in your area, or could you stand a little woodshedding to polish up your talent? Is your library of tunes current, or do you rely on what you've already got in the can?

You are what you believe. Attitude is important. Keep trying out new things until success starts to smack you in the face. You're a professional musician, and you have the inside track. Maybe it's time to expand your horizons beyond the next block. Remember, if you do what you've always done, nothing's going to change. How much do you want better work? How badly do you want to take your career to the next level? Enough to actually do something about it … right away? Those big breaks don't just come out of nowhere. You have to make them happen.

Chapter 2

BUSINESS BASICS

TWO

A Little Bit of
Marketing 101

You're a musician. Maybe you work as a single, maybe you work in a group. Perhaps you specialize in rock, country, big band, or jazz. You know the tunes, you can wail your fanny off, and you just can't wait for the phone to ring with another gig so you can work more. But maybe you don't get as much work as you want. Maybe the phone's not ringing. And maybe those gigs aren't coming in one right after another. You can do one of two things about it.

If they don't know you, where to find you, or how they can reach you—you're out of luck.

1) You can gripe, moan, and complain that nobody appreciates your talents; there's no work out there; clubs won't pay for live music anymore; non-union musicians are scarfing up all the gigs and playing for next to nothing; or DJs are putting a crimp in your business.

2) You can do something about it!

Now, unfortunately, becoming better at playing your instrument does not necessarily mean club owners, agents, and people with money are going to beat a path to your door. Particularly when they don't even know where your door is. So if you're looking for more gigs, or if you want to find better-paying gigs, then you might need more than talent. You have to have a few of the basic necessities, like:

- A promo kit
- A demo video
- Street smarts
- Networking skills
- A demo CD
- Great referrals
- An answering machine or voice mail
- Business cards
- Great references
- A good mailing list
- Computer skills
- A little business savvy
- A telephone or cell phone

In other words, when somebody is looking for a single, a duo, a band, or whatever your niche is, you want them to think of you. And if they don't know you, where to find you, or how to reach you, you're out of luck.

If you are not easily accessible, you won't get the gig.

When the phone's not ringing and the gigs aren't coming, we like to blame it on something like the economy or the weather, but think about what you've done to promote yourself or your group lately. Do you have a press kit? Up-to-date pictures? Creative business cards? A Web site? Should you be in the yellow pages? Do you have a mailing list so when you work in a club, hundreds of people know you're there? Do you have letters of reference, commendations from places you've worked, and a bank of referrals for when things slow down?

When you worked your last gig, did you ask the person who booked you if he knows someone who might also be interested in you and your group? Did you ask if you could use him as a reference?

When people call your phone number, do they get an image of a polished professional or is your phone answered by:

- A four-year-old?   • Your parents?
- A message saying the number is no longer in service?
- An answering machine with a goofy message?
- Nothing … it just rings if you're not there?

If it's any of the above, the problem is basic. When someone decides to book you, they will pick up the phone and call if they know your number. If you're not easily accessible, you won't get the gig. Your job starts with making it easy for the people with the checkbook to find you. It starts with getting your name out there and creating a great image. That gets you in the door. Your playing ability should take it from there. Check it out. What have you done to promote yourself lately?

You Are Only as Good as Your Last Gig

A group I know was hired to play a private party at one of the better hotels in town. It paid well over scale. The people who booked them had heard the band before and were comfortable with their style of music and their choice of tunes. They could play any selection of songs they wanted. Dress was casual—they didn't have to wear tuxedos or even suits. The band had unlimited access to the bar on their breaks. All in all, it was a great gig. A playing job to really look forward to.

Except for one thing. Only a few people showed up. Five hundred invitations had been sent out, but only forty people showed. The weather was awful. A major rainstorm had taken down a number of trees in the area and some power was out—plus there was another major event going on at the same time. To top things off, the city had been hit with a flu epidemic. Everything was going against the people who planned the party. It was painful. There were almost more employees than there were guests.

The party went on almost as planned. But the people who did come only stayed for a short time and the host was visibly embarrassed. The band tried to make the best of a bad situation. But for them, making the best of a bad situation meant starting late, quitting early, taking a lot of breaks, and overdoing it at the bar. As one band member put it, "What did we care? We were still getting paid."

The problem, however, was that one of the people who actually did show was the VP of sales for a major industry in town, a company whose name is a household word. He had verbally committed to using the band at an upcoming dealer conference where the pay was many, many times over scale. He was only there thirty minutes. No one in the band knew he was coming, and they were on a break for twenty of those thirty minutes. When they did play, it was obvious that the drummer had had more than enough to drink. The band simply did not have their hearts in it, and they were goofing around more than actually playing their best charts. The VP left the party—and found another band.

And there lies the moral to this little episode: you're only as good as your last gig. We are musicians. We play live music—we don't play records. We can't just let a CD spin and walk away. We are entertainers, professionals, and musicians who have spent years learning our craft. We want to get paid decent bucks for our talents and skill, and we want our clients to get what they pay for. Actually, more than what they pay for.

Don't cheat the person who hired you or the audience in front of you, no matter what the size. Play like your next gig depends on it. Play for the hotel staff; play for whomever is in your audience.

Don't cheat the person who hired you or the audience in front of you, no matter what the size. Play for yourself. You never know who might be talking about you long after the chairs are piled on the tables and the lights are turned out. It could be an agent, a meeting planner, a club owner, a corporate exec, a hotel manager who books groups, someone who's getting married and looking for a band, a record producer, or maybe just the person who hired you. One dissatisfied person will tell twenty others. Those twenty will tell four hundred, and on it goes.

We've all played gigs where we can't wait for the night to be over and get out the door. Or maybe we've played gigs where they just want "background music," where no one pays any attention to you or your band. But whether you believe it or not, someone is always listening. You never know if that someone could advance your career or put it into a holding pattern.

If you work a single, a little self-discipline can go a long way. If the audience is sparse, make friends with every person in the room. If you're in a band, don't let one irritated musician in your group bring down the whole affair just because it wasn't what you expected. You get paid to play to the best of your ability to a crowd of a thousand, a hundred, or maybe just one. Make it a stellar performance, like your career depended on it. Who knows? It just might.

How to Maximize
Your Bookings

How's your calendar shaping up with playing dates? If your schedule is not as full as you could wish, you might want to do a little soul-searching to examine what you are doing to fill those empty dates. Sitting by the phone is not enough; you have to get it to ring. You have to find people to talk to. You need to expand your customer base and let people know how to find you when they need you or your group.

Here are twenty things to check to make sure you're maximizing the possibilities of booking that next gig.

1) Check your business cards. Do you even have them? Do you have enough? Does your card stand out from everyone else's? Is all the information current? Do you have your e-mail and Web site addresses on your card? Is it a good-looking billboard for your musical services?

2) Update your promo kit. Those testimonials from five years ago may still work, but the ones from the past twelve months will work better. Do those photos actually look like you or more like your high school yearbook picture?

3) Update your Web site. Do you have a Web site? If you don't, get one up, or have someone do it for you right away. If you're going to compete in the music business, you can't be without one. See what your competition is doing, and then do something better. Provide cuts from your demo CD, or a piece from your demo video. Make it look like you're a major player.

4) Throw out the $29 answering machine and get something that makes you sound as professional as you are. Try using voice mail if your local phone company provides it.

5) Get a video of you working a gig, or update the one you have now. Make sure your name and phone number are on the label and on the video. Be sure the phone number is correct.

6) Send out a mailer to let people know where they can catch you playing on a regular basis. This includes mailing to all your past clients, and all the great leads in your database. (You do have a database, don't you?)

7) Do you have decent letterhead and envelopes? Make sure you look as good in print as you actually are. Send postcards with your picture in full color to three past clients each day and ask for referrals. Hey, you never know.

Make sure you look as good in print as you do in person.

8) Call six different people every day just to say hello. Ask these people if they know someone who could use your services. You'll be surprised how many leads you get.

9) Staple your business card to every bill you pay by mail. They will see your name and what you do, even if they just throw the card away. Any visibility helps.

10) Check your pricing. How much do you charge? Are you pricing yourself in the "best-seller" category or the "bargain bin" category? Are you getting what you're worth? Are you doing well or just getting by? Do people book you just because you're cheap? Or if they pay a lot more, are they getting the best? You know

your market. At least you'd better know it. Time to check it out again. If you're not losing at least a gig a month because of price, you're not charging enough.

11) Clean up your act. Is your instrument the best you want it to be? Is your equipment up to date? Do you have the best in lights, audio, and effects? How about your clothes? Could your appearance stand to be updated as well?

12) Tweak your material. Constantly update your tunes. Keep in touch with what's going on in today's music scene; know what's hot and what's not. Listen to all types of music, not just what you like personally.

If you're not losing at least a gig a month because of price, you're not charging enough.

13) Subscribe to trade magazines, music magazines, and read the *International Musician*. Keep current. Know what's going on around you. Read books on marketing, self-promotion, and sales strategies. Getting better gigs doesn't simply mean having a great axe or better equipment. The music business is a marketing business. Find out what other people do to create more customer contact.

14) Tell everyone what you do. You never know where that next gig is going to come from.

15) Never quote a price for a gig on the phone without first finding out who's calling. They don't always book you on the phone right away. You need a name and phone number to call back. Never end the call without trying to close a definite date. Don't give a price and let the caller say, "I'll get back to you." Get specifics. Find out what it will take to book the gig.

16) Have a print piece on yourself—one that you can fit in a #10 envelope. Don't send five pounds of promo material right away; test the waters first. You can also carry these smaller pieces/brochures around with you like business cards, so when you're at the supermarket and see someone who needs your services, say, "Here's my card—and my brochure, too!" Always be prepared.

17) Don't start hacking away at your fee if somebody says, "Your price is too high." First, explain the benefits of using your services: your talent, your experience, your past performances. Success breeds success. You can always go down in price later and still make decent money.

18) Do a few gigs for charities. Use them as opportunities to meet fellow musicians.

19) Don't let a bad gig get you down. If the last gig was the pits, don't let it ruin your enthusiasm. People will hear it in your voice when they talk to you. Clients want to book musicians who are excited about their services.

20) Network your way to success. It's not who you know, it's who can you know. Expand your circle of influence. Ask every person who books you for a gig if you can use him or her as a reference. They might even suggest promising leads. Don't be afraid to ask.

Remember, you are in the entertainment business. It's a fun business. Your attitude will get you as many gigs as your talent, marketing expertise, and sales skills. But it's a combination of all of the above that will get you more gigs, fun gigs, and better-paying gigs as well.

Treat Your Band
Like a Business

Your band is like the record store, the grocery story, or the business down the street. They all vie for the same customers. There are only so many customers and they want to get their share. The same goes for bands. There are a lot of bands and only so many jobs. So what makes a club, promoter, wedding party, or meeting planner choose one group or single over another?

The answer might not be exactly what you think. There are many excellent groups made up of excellent musicians. Many bands are very good, play great tunes, have a solid reputation, and are well liked. So in the case of everything being equal talent-wise, which band ends up with the gig? More often than not, it's the band with the best business chops.

Here's an inside look on how some professional musicians are able to get an above-average amount of work on a regular basis. These are groups that are constantly up against other bands and get more than their share of gigs, particularly from:

1) Major companies planning to have musical entertainment at their next corporate event.

2) Couples getting married who are searching for someone to play for their wedding reception.

3) Club owners or managers looking for a single or duo, either for a one-time gig or for a regular engagement.

4) Concert promoters scoping out local talent for a major show.

In all cases, there are plenty of groups and musicians up for consideration.

Many times companies planning corporate events have home offices that are 1,000 or more miles away. They book bands that have great demo videos, have glowing references, but also have an 800 number. It is easy to contact them, someone always answers the phone, and they feel like the group is right next door. Remember, an 800 number is no longer expensive; you can pay by the call, and it makes it easy for people to get in touch with you. It also separates you from groups whose phone numbers change on a regular basis, and an 800 number can be the same whenever or wherever you move.

How easy are you to book? Couples who are looking for a band to play at their wedding have their pick of dozens of groups. Many times the ones selected are those that take credit cards. If the wedding budget cash flow is starting to run a little short, they can conveniently put it on a credit card. Also, if you're selling CDs, T-shirts, or anything else, it's something you might want to consider. Accepting credit cards makes it much easier to sell merchandise over the phone or on the Web. Get set up with your local bank. Make your group easy to buy.

You want to give the impression of a stable group that will actually show up for the gig.

Sometimes the managers of country clubs book band six months or more in advance. One of their biggest fears is that the single or group won't be around that far down the road. Just like the local business who advertises "Since 1940," you want to give the impression of a stable group that will actually show up for the gig. No one wants to book a group only to find out six months later they aren't together any more. Play up the fact that you're reliable. Use an AFM contract to show you're a professional who means business.

Most of the time concert promoters don't want just another band. They want a group who has a big mailing list, whose name will lend credibility to the program, and who have good pictures (full color, and black and white) of the group that can be used in the advertising. A Polaroid or amateurish photo just doesn't work. So the message here is very clear. Look professional by having professional photos taken of you and your group, and by putting together a database of people who come to hear you play. It's never too late to start. These are great selling tools.

Sometimes being a great musician or playing with a great group is not enough. Treat your band like a business. Think outside the box. Flaunt your union card. Act like the professional you are. Then find out what it's going to take to get that next booking. What can you do to separate yourself from everyone else?

Whether your target is corporate entertainment, the club scene, or concert venues, determine what it is that makes your band the best choice. Capitalize on your own uniqueness, and let everybody know you're perfect for that next high-paying gig.

Word-of-Mouth Marketing
for Professional Musicians

If you asked 100 people who play music for a living what their best means of marketing and promotion is, more than 90 percent would say, "word of mouth." And if you asked these musicians what word of mouth is, only a few could tell you exactly what they mean. Some believe it means sitting back, doing nothing, and waiting for people to magically seek you out. That is, of course, ludicrous. Successful word-of-mouth marketing needs constant attention on your part. It means constant tweaking of ideas to get your name out there, coming up with reasons for people to talk about you in a positive manner, and staying in touch with your own personal circle of influence.

First of all, word-of-mouth marketing starts with knowing your craft. Nothing gets the ball rolling faster than playing really well. With a band, it means having a tight group, with talent as good as it gets. You're only as good as your last performance, and a well-received playing job keeps that word of mouth going.

But not everyone can hear you play all the time. Not everyone knows of your successes and achievements. Not everyone knows where you are playing all the time. And that's where some coaxing is necessary to keep that positive spin going. The nice part of word-of-mouth marketing is that it costs nothing. You don't have to spend big dollars on CDs, press kits, and promo packages. You just have to keep the right people saying the right things about you.

Being a professional musician means treating your career like a business. It means constant networking. It means letting everyone you come in contact with know that you are a professional musician. And it means creating a constant buzz to keep people talking about you. Creating that buzz through word of mouth is what helps to keep you working.

It's easy to create a buzz for any kind of music you play. You could be a country group, hard rock or heavy metal band, cocktail piano player, or symphonic string musician. The idea here is to tell everyone you come in contact with where you are playing. Let them know you're a musician. It could be your local dry cleaner, druggist, or a FedEx delivery person. Doesn't matter. If you come in contact with this person on a regular basis, say, "By the way, we're playing at the Whatever Club this week; come see us. We've been getting excellent reviews." Ask if they could mention it to their friends. Next thing you know they are telling their friends that "the musician who plays at the Whatever Club" is someone they know and they've heard the group "has

> **The idea here is to tell everyone you come in contact with where and when you are going to be playing.**

been getting excellent reviews." Even if they haven't heard you play, they can still spread the word. If you play with the local symphony, let everyone you interact with know. Don't just hand them a schedule; let them know what you play, and the date of the next concert. Create some PR on your own. If your band has won an award or you will be performing at Carnegie Hall, let people know the good news. Word spreads. Your phone could easily start ringing for freelance work because you're "the violinist who is playing with the symphony at Carnegie Hall." Starting your own buzz is real word-of-mouth marketing.

If you treat your music career as a business, you probably have one or two sets of business cards. It could be as a soloist or as a group. An easy way to promote yourself through word of mouth is to staple your business card to every bill you pay by mail. A person has to see your card, even if it is just to take it off and throw it away. Do this month after month, and I bet people will start talking about you down at the phone company, utility company, or department store credit office. ("Here's that guitar player again—hand me the staple puller.") At least they're talking about you.

Also, don't forget about local call-in radio shows, and the opinion page of your local paper. They're great venues for keeping your buzz going. If you have a take on the local music that is even slightly controversial, it could work in your favor. Get known as an expert in the area, and people will talk about you. Getting your name out through word-of-mouth marketing is easy, it's cheap, and it works if you're creative and continually work to keep it going. Remember this: people will spread your buzz if it is simple to repeat and interesting enough to get attention. How you come up with it is up to you. Then fan the flames once in a while to keep it going. If you're a great musician, word spreads fast. But it only keeps spreading if you seed it yourself on a regular basis. That's what word-of-mouth marketing is all about.

Do You Need
a Record Company?

Do you need a record company? It is really up to you. It depends on what you are trying to accomplish. The answer is yes if you are looking for high visibility, widespread distribution, and a small (sometimes very small) percentage of sales. The answer is no if you can develop your own marketing, can handle your own distribution, and want a major portion of the profits.

If you think the answer is yes, it takes quite a bit of work. You need to deal with a record company's Artist and Repertoire (A&R) person and get him or her on your side. In order to make yourself signable, you have to appear to be already signed. Your recordings have to be great; they have to be absolutely first-rate. You're not going to do this with a bunch of songs recorded on a cheap tape recorder with a lyric sheet printed in longhand. Your CDs and lyric sheets have to look totally professional, and your press and bio materials have to be of the same quality the record company department heads are used to seeing. You need to create your own press, get reviewed, and have a loyal following. In fact, an A&R person was once asked by a group how to meet A&R people. The answer was, "Create a buzz, generate press, and acquire a following—and we'll find you."

You need to create your own press, get reviewed, and have a loyal following.

It's good to have help on the PR side of things. A professional print shop to help you put together photos and graphics helps too. If you have substandard material, you're going to have a tough time convincing anyone you're worth signing. A&R people don't want to do a lot of your work for you. The less work they have to do, the easier it is to get them to sign you. And even if your stuff is first-rate, be prepared to hear a lot of noes and deal with rejection as well as a small return for your efforts if your record doesn't hit the charts.

Now, if you don't think you need (or want to use) a record company, there are other ways to go. With the advent of the Internet, the whole recording industry is going through a dramatic change. CDs are starting to be replaced by minidiscs, an even more compact technology using credit-card-sized receptacles that hold compressed MP3 files downloaded from the Internet. This really levels the playing field. Independent labels have the same presence as the majors on the Internet. Only problem is, people have to know about your songs, either through search engines or by word of mouth. They need something to inspire them to want to hear and buy your songs. It is estimated that more than 60 percent of record purchases are unplanned. That's why record stores have listening posts, use point-of-purchase advertising, and spend megabucks on promotion.

People have to know your songs through search engines or by word of mouth.

Today you can buy CDs on-line, in record stores, in department stores, in gift shops, in airports, in restaurants, through mail-order, and just about anywhere there's customer traffic. This is where niche marketing has its place. If your group has a small but devoted audience, you could do very well without a major label contract. You could start your own. If you've got a following, a mailing list, and some marketing smarts, you could do very well. You could specialize in Irish songs, polkas, Jewish party music, or military marches and sell a lot of CDs. I have a friend who has a great polka group, but record stores won't give him a place for his CDs on their racks. He came up with his own label and markets directly to his 200,000-name mailing list. (These are either the people who went to hear him play over the past fifteen years or just those he came in contact with.) He came out with a "best of" CD, did a two-piece mailing to his list, and sold 35,000 CDs. He got the lion's share of the profits instead of a small percentage. Granted, he didn't get on *Billboard's* Top 40 chart with a bullet, but he made a ton of money.

If you create original music and can define, target, and market to a specific audience, you may want to consider an independent label. For an artist to accrue the same income on a major label, millions of records would need to be sold. But you don't get the fame and visibility with your own label and marketing efforts. That's why you have to decide for yourself which route you're going to take.

One of the benefits of belonging to the AFM is that they have recording contracts available to use and a pension plan in place. Many musicians have found that the shooting star to record success turned out to be a Roman candle and came down in flames. So go carefully. Decide if a record company is what you need. If it is, determine what you actually want to accomplish before searching for one.

Ten Questions You Should Ask Yourself Before Taking Your Band on the Road

Pulling up stakes and taking your band on the road takes some serious thought. It also takes sacrifice and money. If you don't take it seriously, it could be the end of your group. You could wind up hundreds or even thousands of miles from home, stranded with little more than gas money, not knowing where your next gig is coming from. Taking playing jobs away from home on a week-after-week basis has to be treated like a business trip, not as a fun time hanging out with your musician friends. You need to control your expenses, file union contracts to make sure you'll get paid, know there will be enough work, and have some long-term goals in mind. I did an on-line survey of things to consider, and found you should ask yourself these ten questions before hitting the road.

> **Away jobs have to be treated as a business trip, not as a fun time hanging out with some friends.**

1) Have you exhausted all the possibilities of places to play in your area? Have you saturated your own market? If you live in a big city like Los Angeles, Las Vegas, or New York, the opportunities for constant local work are much better than in Fresno, Binghamton, or Dubuque. If the work is still coming in, you're regularly making decent bucks, and you're able to sleep in your own bed at the same time, you might want to think carefully about long-distance gigs.

2) What is your goal? Do you want to get more exposure, sell some CDs, break into the "big time," create extra revenue for yourself, or get valuable experience? In fact, do you have a goal at all? This is not a time for you to shoot from the hip. Do you

have a plan? Where do you see yourself six months or a year from now? What are you doing to achieve that goal?

3) How are you going to get there? Do you have reliable transportation? Are you taking more than one car? Do you need a truck, or can you get by with a couple of cars and a trailer? Depending on the size of the group, and heavy gear, traveling groups usually require more than just a couple of seats in the car and a big trunk.

4) Are you and your band members ready to make a commitment to give up a day job and head out? Do you know enough booking agents, club owners, and other contacts who can keep you going when things slow down?

5) Do you have the best possible press kit, pictures, demo CD and video, Web site, endorsements, and mailing list? Is your mailing list divided by area? If you want the people in the music industry to take you seriously, a professional image is a must. You are not going to make it with a demo cassette tape and a box of business cards.

6) Do you have the right type of instruments and pro gear that can take the abuse of being on the road? Do you have the right cases to transport everything safely week after week? Do you have enough backup equipment and accessories for when things break down?

7) Do you have great networking skills? This is Business Basics 101. Being on the road is as much about who you know as it is who knows you.

8) Do you have enough cash and credit cards to keep you going when (or if) the well starts to run dry? Food and motels are a necessity, not a luxury. You need places to stay between gigs, and you need to be able to pay for them when you're looking for a new club if a gig you were counting on suddenly evaporates.

9) Are there groups like yours working constantly? Is there enough demand for your type of music to keep you booked regularly? Is your group mainstream enough to keep your calendar full?

10) The last question you have to ask yourself is, "Am I good enough?" Are you as good as or better than the groups in your field out there? It doesn't matter if you are a cover band, polka band, country group, hard-rock band, or jazz ensemble. If you decide to leave town and make a living playing music on the road, your chops had better be there. Your band must be tight. You need to look good, sound great, be professional, and have a tremendous amount of business savvy. It's a very competitive world out there.

You need to look your best, sound great, and be business savvy.

Taking your band out on the road in this day and age is not for the faint of heart. But there's money to be made. Even though clubs are closing or not using bands like they used to, new ones are opening up. There is still private work in corporate venues. There are fairs and large music events. There are a lot of places to play, but you have to be wired for it. Think it over carefully before you set out on the road.

Web Sites: You're Going to Need One Sooner or Later

You can play with the best. You've got your axe down cold. You know all the tunes. You've got the best professional audio gear, you've got personality to spare, and the audiences love you. So why isn't your phone ringing off the hook? Perhaps the business cards you tacked to the local grocery store bulletin board are not enough. Maybe it's time for an Internet presence. All the better groups and musicians have one. If you don't have one already, it's time to get your feet wet.

Personally, I'm not extremely computer literate. I don't have the slightest idea how to set up a Web site. I have people who do it for me. Maybe it's a generation thing. But you can learn. If you are older, ask your kids for help. A Web site can be a virtual press kit. The amount of information you can post on your Web site is huge, and you can always expand on it. Instead of sending a package through the mail with a press kit, pictures, and a CD, you can just tell your potential client to check out your Web site. It's easy to do, and you can make it look impressive. You don't have to send it FedEx or UPS. They get it immediately, at no delivery charge to you.

Beyond the basics of who you are, you can impress, dazzle, and intrigue check-book-holding customers with your Web site.

Today you can use programs like RealAudio or Liquid Audio to utilize the magic of streaming. You can even have video, so your client can see and hear you in action. The neat part of having a Web site for yourself or your band is that there are endless possibilities for what you can put on your site. Beyond the basics (who you are, what you play, how to contact you, and where you are playing), you can impress, dazzle, and intrigue checkbook-holding customers. You'll be able to get your calendar filled with great playing dates in no time.

Whether you like it or not the Internet is not going away. The sooner you jump in, the more you and your group will benefit from the magic of today's technology. So for right now, let's fast-forward to the part where you're convinced you need a Web site, you figure out how to do it yourself or get some help, and you're up and running at whatever domain name you choose.

First, check out other bands' Web sites. Think of how you can do something different to make your site stand out. Be sure to ask all the people you play with who have a Web site to include a link to yours somewhere on their pages. Search engines such as Alta Vista, Lycos, and Yahoo! will include you in their directories if you ask them. Have a listing of when and where you'll be playing. But don't just list all the gigs you've got coming up, include all the places you've played in the past as well. Highlight the famous people you've worked with. You can even detail all the equipment you own and the instruments you play.

One thing you might want to consider is to put your group in an online band listing that will link to your Web site. You can also get linked to some fraternity or college links if you're a party band. Just be a little creative. If your band has CDs or you have your own T-shirts, you can sell them on your site.

Then, of course, you have to get traffic to your site. You need people to look at it. So put the address of your site on your business cards and on any print material you might have. Get your page linked to other sites. You need to have something unique that makes it to the top in major search engines under your name, the name of your group, the style of music you play, and any other way people can identify you.

Computers are here to stay. If it was up to me, I would still have rotary dial phones with flashing hold buttons, and a big yellow legal pad with a bunch of #2 pencils. But those days are gone. No one can afford to be computer free or computer illiterate. When the parade passes you've got to march or you'll be left behind.

A good Web site can open a lot of doors.

A good Web site can open a lot of doors, no matter what style of music you play, or wherever you live. It can be the most fun and profitable conduit between you and your fans, you and your clients, or you and the world.

Booking Your Own Club Dates

Maybe you don't have an agent, or maybe the phone isn't quite ringing off the hook to book you or your band. Whether you're a single or a cover band, in jazz or rock, just having a great sound is not always going to cut it. Getting work takes an awful lot of your time, plus it takes patience and persistence. You're also going to have to invest a few bucks to be that "overnight success." There's no real secret to getting those casual date gigs. But it takes more than musicianship. If you want to get the better-paying jobs, here's a little checklist of things you need.

1) An up-to-date press package. You do have one, don't you? You need a three- or four-song CD, recent photos, a list of places where you've performed, and a quote sheet with important comments about you (if you're a single), your band, and your music. Make sure that those endorsements are from credible people. The more well-known names you can come up with, the easier it will be to sell your group. A short video is also great for getting casual dates, because they can see how good you look as well as how good you sound. And don't forget a personalized cover letter to whomever you're sending your press kit.

Getting work takes time, patience, and persistence.

2) A song list. Don't skip this part. If you're a cover band, lounge act, or cocktail pianist, you have to be prepared to do as many as four or five sets a night. You want easily recognized, familiar tunes, and you want whoever is booking you to know you have a terrific repertoire.

3) Business cards. That's obvious. Make sure your cards have up-to-date area and zip codes, maybe a four-color picture of you

or your group, and a line or two about what makes you special. You don't want the name of every member of your band and their phone number on the card. One name, one phone number. Make it easy. Give it some class if that's your thing, or some creativeness if you're more hip.

4) An answering machine. C'mon, you can't sit around your house all day waiting for the phone to ring. And you can't afford to miss any calls. Be diligent about checking your machine, and get back to those people right away. You might also consider a pager. When somebody is interested in booking you, they want info right away. Not tomorrow. Not next week. Today.

5) A pocket-sized calendar you always have with you. If somebody decides on the spot to book you or your group, you don't want to have to check your calendar back at home. Keep it with you and up to date.

6) Check to see if the venue is right for you. Do some research. Are you the type of single or group the club usually books? If you're a ten-piece group expected to play on a three-piece stage, there are going to be some problems. If you're a jazz group that's trying to fit into a more commercial or rock club, you might get people walking out. How about age of clientele? Do you fit?

7) A thick skin. In order to get one casual date gig, you're going to have to make a lot of contacts, and send out a lot of stuff. Not everyone who gets your CD and press kit will run to the phone to book you. Many will forget who you are when you call. ("I never saw that envelope, can you send it again?") You have to

be able to handle a little rejection and being brushed off. Don't settle for "We'll get back to you" and expect them actually to get back. It doesn't work that way. A decent amount of persistence can work wonders.

8) Contracts. That's where being a union musician is an advantage. Your local supplies them. Use them. Get that signature on the dotted line. Then when you show up for work, you have some recourse if the lights are out or they didn't remember they booked you.

Show some personality and a positive attitude.

9) Some personality. You're good. You know it. Let everyone else know as well. But do it with a little charm and personality. Keep a positive attitude when talking to whomever is booking you for that casual date. Don't start to get testy if things don't go your way or if you don't get the gig. These people have friends. And if they don't like your temperament, they'll tell them all.

10) Thank-you notes. Other singles or groups seldom send them. After the gig is over, send the club or person who booked you a note of thanks. It doesn't have to be long. It could be handwritten. It will set you apart from everyone else they hire.

There's the list. How do you stack up? Sometimes forgetting the obvious things can cost us a gig or two. The music business is also a marketing business. It's not just another couple of practice sessions that bring the work in. You need to continue to keep up-to-date on both.

Success
Breeds Success

The easiest way to become successful in the music business is to appear already successful. Nobody really wants to hire someone who seems not to have had a playing job in months. Anyone who hires musicians wants to book bands or singles that are currently working, are in demand, and are well established. Maybe your calendar isn't as full as you'd like it to be, but don't let a prospective check writer know. The old rule of not airing your dirty laundry in public applies here, too.

You're a professional. Act like it. If your van broke down this morning and you don't have the bucks to fix it, don't complain to someone you hope will book you. If your spouse decided to leave you with the kids, or if your guitar just got stolen when you left **You're a** your car unlocked, let's not let that corporate meeting **professional** planner know about it when discussing a potential date. **—act like it.** If you just replaced two of the guys in your band because they had trigger tempers and were going at each other, don't broadcast it. Think about this: you don't want to tell people your problems because 80 percent of those people don't care, and the rest are glad you have them. You want to appear as if you have all the work in the world, are really good at what you do, and are very cool and collected about it.

If a club wants to hear you on tape or CD before thinking about booking you, don't give them something you made with a $25 tape recorder. And don't give them photos of your group shot with a cheap disposable camera either. Images are important. Would you want a doctor to operate on you if he came into the operating room wearing a ratty T-shirt and dirty jeans?

74

Recently, I had a call from a fairly well-known vocalist who is changing keyboard players. The reason was that this person was the prophet of doom and always complained to customers on the breaks about how the smoke was making him sick, the lack of decent work in the area, and how he was tired of playing the same old tunes every night. Here's a talented musician who could work steadily, yet whines and complains his way through life. Club owners don't want to hear it. Neither do customers or your fellow musicians. Keep it to yourself. You'll get more work.

Looking successful doesn't just mean owning state-of-the-art equipment. Even the best union musicians don't upgrade constantly, or need to spend the bucks. It does mean having a good-looking brochure with great references, sounding good with demo CDs and videos, and

Appear to be successful— even if you are not yet.

having an attitude that makes people think you are successful, even if you're not quite there yet. It means using and filing a union contract. Handshake agreements don't work here. Get it in writing. A contract is binding and shows professionalism.

The music business is a fun business, and the more gigs you get, and the more money you make, the more fun it can be. Here's a little checklist for gauging how well you're doing.

Ask yourself how often you use these phrases:
- "I haven't had a gig that payed above scale in a year."
- "There's no work here. People want musicians to play for free."
- "Man, nobody wants to hire bands anymore."
- "Do you need a band? We're out of work right now."
- "Of course we can play, we have nothing else coming up."

It would be a lot better to be saying:
- "I think we can fit this gig into our schedule and give you just what you're looking for."
- "Let me check my book to see if that date is still available."
- "We play that type of venue a lot for clients, and can do a great job for you."
- "I can send you a press kit and demo CD, but let me know quick before the date gets booked."

Success breeds success. If you come across as an accomplished, successful, well-rounded, personable musician with a good attitude, the odds are that people will be much more anxious to pay more for you to perform. Act successful, even if you're not yet. To get better work, you have to appear to be already working. Play the part. Success is sure to follow.

Chapter 3

SELF-PROMOTION

First You've Got to Get Their Attention

I remember when I first started out in the music business, I would do anything to get publicity or a booking for my band. If there was a club we really wanted to play and couldn't get the owner's attention to book us, or even call us back, we would call the club as customers and ask if our group was playing there. After a few similar calls, I'd casually stop by and leave a card. Usually the owner or manager would say, "I think I've heard of you guys." Of course they'd heard of us. We were the ones making the calls.

Another little exercise was mailing our group's brochure to whomever was looking for a band (in a plain envelope with no return address). On the brochure was a little note that read, "Hi

If people don't know about you, they won't hire you.

____. You should hear these guys, they're fantastic!" Then we'd just sign the note with a generic first name like John or Bob—everybody has a friend named John or Bob. I guess I would do any crazy thing I could to get someone to book my group.

If people don't know about you, they won't hire you. But sometimes getting them just to know about you isn't enough. You need to get them to take action: listen to your CDs, look at your promo kit, even check out your band at a current gig.

One booking agent jokingly said, "Maybe you could take off your clothes and run down Main Street naked. When they arrest you, you can tell the press your band's playing wherever, and you've got CDs available as well. At least you'll get noticed, and they might want to hear what you sound like."

Today, playing out is not my main career, but I marvel at the moxie some groups show when they're working to get gigs. They try really hard and don't fear rejection. In fact, I like anybody who can come up with a great idea for getting noticed.

Personality skills, creativeness, and cleverness do pay off when you are trying to book a gig. I know someone who laminates their business card to a dollar bill and gives it out to serious agents or club owners. That business card seldom gets thrown out. Most people don't take the time to get a razor blade and try to remove the dollar, but they also don't want to throw a dollar in the wastebasket. It hangs around forever.

If you're trying to get more wedding gigs or private parties, stapling your business card to every bill you pay by mail could have an effect (I mentioned this before and it works). A human being has to see your name, even if it's just to throw the card away. And if the conversation ever turns to the subject of needing a band, they might remember you or your group. Visibility is important, and anything you can do without spending money is the key.

> **Visibility is important—anything you can do without spending money is key.**

I know of a local band that sends out a letter with a Japanese Yen rubber cemented to the top of the page. It reads, "We've got a Yen to play your next party." Yen coins cost next to nothing. And I bet the letter gets read. How about this? Send your prospect a cassette tape (not a CD) in an envelope with the message: "This tape will self-destruct in ten seconds" printed on the outside of the envelope. Whoever opens the package will listen to the tape right away. And instead of the "Mission: Impossible" theme, they'll hear you and your group with info on how to book you. You also might want to think about putting your group's picture on your business cards. People want to see what musicians look like. Full-color cards are relatively inexpensive today. Pictures make a strong impact.

You should have a mailing list of people who will come to hear your group wherever you are playing. But you also need a mailing list of people who might possibly book you. And you need to stay in touch with these people on a regular basis. It could be something as simple as a postcard letting them know where you're playing or a phone call in the middle of the afternoon when you're more apt to get an answering machine. Then you just leave the message, "Got good news for you. Please give me a call." Everybody likes good news. It could be that you have an open date, can supply a mailing list of 2,000 people that might come hear you, or have added something different to your play list.

Find ways to get their attention so they will call you back.

You never know where the next creative idea for getting someone's attention is going to come from. It could be from a friend, a fellow musician, another band, or even a business down the street. Use a little ingenuity. When a gig you thought you had falls through, or people booking musicians start to look elsewhere, maybe there's a way to keep it from happening again. Maybe it's just a matter of getting that person to hear you one more time. Maybe you need to get their attention and find ways to get them to call you back.

If you depend on club dates and freelance gigs for an income, then it's a business. It takes more than just musical talent. You need to get your name out there, and you need to create attention for yourself. A little cleverness and creativity never hurt.

Selling Yourself to Increase Bookings

Getting more gigs means being able to sell yourself and your band. You need some sales chops. I read an interesting quote in an article on George Forman, the heavyweight boxing champion. George stated, "I learned something early in life. If you know how to sell yourself, you'll never starve. In any profession, you can find yourself out on the street, saying, 'They don't want me anymore.' But if you have some selling skills, you will never go hungry." It's true. The only problem is, to be really good at selling you have to want to do it. A lot of musicians aren't good at selling themselves or their group because they just don't want to have to "sell." They don't like it. They think they're not wired for it.

The nice part about promoting your group is realizing you're really in the entertainment industry. It's a great business. You add excitement, happiness, and enjoyment to people's lives. And the more money you can make, the more fun it can be for you. To be really good at selling yourself and your group, you have to continually relearn your skills. You can't become complacent. You need to practice your selling skills regularly, just like you work on your music chops every day. Remember, "while you're green you're growing, when you're ripe you rot." Keep that in mind. You can always learn something new, or remember something you may have forgotten. You have to keep an open mind.

If you know how to sell yourself, you'll never starve.

Selling yourself and your band takes a certain amount of assertiveness. There are those who use the "I don't push" approach. "If you don't want to book me now, call me when you're ready, here's my card." It's a great tactic if you don't mind making less money. The other end of the spectrum is the "This is how I make my living, so I'm going to stay in your face until you book me" approach to selling. These people usually do pretty well, except that the amount of verbal abuse they have to take doesn't necessarily make life pleasant. And if your music career isn't fun, what's the point?

Don't despair—there is a happy medium. It's not pressure. It's more like exercising a certain amount of decent persistence. With some potential bookers, you can use a lot. With others, even a small amount can be too much. If you talk to someone who might book you on the phone, be sure to send some promotional material, call him or her again, and set up a meeting. If they don't book you, you have to stay in their face if you want to end up booking the gig. You can't let them hang up, send them a card, and then expect them to be calling you the next day. It doesn't work that way. Sure, people say, "We'll get back to you." Sometimes they lie. Well, maybe a few call back, but they're the exception rather than the rule.

Let me share with you a couple of ideas that some musicians who earn an above-average income use to book more gigs. They don't let club owners hang up and hope for the best. They persist until they at least get a clear no. Here is one approach a musician in southern California uses when he quotes a gig and the person doesn't book it right away. He always gets their name and phone number, and calls them during the day when an answering machine might be on. He leaves a message to the effect that he forgot to tell them something important about his group, and please call him as soon as they can. He might follow it up with a postcard a few days later saying, "Give me a call, I've got good news for you." He says the more times he talks to the person, the closer he is to the gig. And the quicker he can get the client to call him back, the easier it is to book the date.

Another approach a musician in Florida uses to get a club owner or client to call back is to entice them with something for free. A couple of CDs, table tents, posters, a special mailer to local fans, whatever. You just want to get them to call you back one more time. Obviously you're not going to exert all this effort if it is a nothing gig. But if it's a gig that pays decent bucks, you have to use a certain amount of pressure salesmanship. That is, of course, if you really want to get the job.

> **The quicker you can get them to call you back, the easier it is to book the date.**

And that's what it comes down to. How badly do you want to book the job? Particularly when the club owner or customer says, "Look, I want to think about it. I like your group, but I want to check my schedule. Send me a promo kit. Send me your latest CD, I'll kick it around." Let's not give up. Go after them. Call. Write. Ask them to stop in where you're currently playing. If you're their friend, they won't mind a little constant contact. And you are their friend, aren't you? If you're not, you might have to go back to square one. The whole idea is this: if you really want to increase your bookings dramatically, get those people who said, "I'll think about it" on the phone one more time. Be persistent until they book you or say no. You just never know...they might say yes!

Primitive Promotions When You're Starting from Scratch

Are you a band that is just starting out? Or maybe you're a group that just hasn't hit their stride yet. Have you found that you just don't have the bucks to promote your group and are trying to do it on an already-tight budget? Where do you turn? What do you do? Here are a couple of options.

First of all, if you've got any club work coming up, or are in negotiation for gigs, remember that these people could help you get through the bleak periods. You're a professional, and are going to get a signed contract. But that in itself doesn't get you any cash right now. Maybe you need lighting equipment, a better sound system, or something as simple as business cards. If your credit cards are maxed, one idea is to ask for a deposit along with the contract. If your gig is for $2,000, maybe you could ask for 25 percent in advance. If the club owner balks, you could explain that you're going to use the money for better equipment for his gig, and he'll benefit from it in the long run. Or you could just say that the gig is so far in the future you need the deposit to secure the date.

Make sure you ask for a deposit along with the contract.

You have to be careful, though, if the date is right around the corner. One band tried this when the job was just a few days away. They were to be paid $1,200, and the club was 100 miles away. The owner said he always paid in cash, but agreed to give them a check for $300 in advance. They played the gig, got $900 in cash, and then the deposit check bounced. You have to be a little careful—some club owners' checks are dependent on the day's take.

When you finally get your first gig, or are starting to get some regular gigs, make sure you maintain decent relationships with the club owners. When the job is done, take the opportunity to lay the groundwork for your future. Ask the owner about other bookings.

One thing you might eventually do about generating return bookings is to insert a return engagement clause in your contracts. Just be careful not to commit yourself too far in advance. You never know what good turns of fortune may lie down the road, and you don't want to be tied to some low-money dates once you've taken your band to the next level.

If you know the club is booked for a while, tell them you are also booked, but would like to discuss the possibility of returning in six weeks, or even a bit longer. Mention that you enjoyed working there, but (and this is a very important "but") also ask the owner to write a letter of recommendation for you. Tell him or her that this is one of the first jobs you've played, or one of the best jobs you've played, so you'd like a letter saying that you did a good job, that the crowd was receptive, that it was an excellent revenue night, and that you showed up on time. You also would like it to say that he or she plans to hire you again at the earliest opportunity. Put it in your own words, but make them think it was their idea. Maybe you could even write it yourself on club letterhead and ask the club owner to simply sign it. Some club owners hate the idea of writing a recommendation letter, but will agree to it if you do it for them.

A portfolio of recommendations is a great asset in getting jobs.

A portfolio of recommendations is of great value in getting jobs. Auditioning is tough. When a prospective employer reads that five clubs found you prompt and good at playing danceable sets, that you've increased attendance by an average of 25 percent, and that you've been offered return bookings, you could be a lot closer to getting more work.

Something else—club owners know each other. They know which bands are a pain to work with, and which ones compliment the club. When you're done with a gig for a particular club (whether a one-nighter or a series of engagements), ask the owner about other job possibilities, either in town or out of town. These people know the business. If they like you, they are more apt to refer you, or just give you a couple of names and have you go for yourself.

Constant communication at this point is very important. Some club owners don't like to return calls (surprise, surprise). If you don't hear from them, don't give up. Send them a note. Give them another call. Leave an interesting message on their answering machine. Call them again. A little persistence can have a big payoff. Use your personality. Get them to like you, and ask them to book you. Even if they don't book you, always let them know where you are playing, what you are doing, and how you could do a great job for them if the opportunity presents itself.

A little persistence can have a big payoff.

The right breaks in the club and casual-date business are the breaks you make for yourself. When you are just starting out, or before you get any kind of a name for yourself, you need to make your own success. A little primitive promotion and some marketing smarts really help.

The Stay-in-Their-Face Approach to Booking More Gigs

I know a club owner who books bands on weekends. I was talking to him about various groups he uses, and asked if a certain group that played there last year would be coming back. He said he thought that they had either broken up or moved out of town. I told him I had just heard them play at a local venue, and his response was, "Well, they haven't been staying in my face." Believe it or not, sometimes it takes some constant contact to get booked again. And sometimes it takes more than one or two attempts to secure a gig at a local club, corporate venue, or casual date.

Sometimes it takes constant contact to get booked again at a club.

The problem is we hate to leave messages and not have calls returned. We don't want to hear "no" because rejection can be hard to take. I was surprised to hear booking agents say they would rather have someone call too much than not enough. Again, they would rather have someone "stay-in-their-face." I guess the trick is to know where that fine line of annoyance versus decent persistence is.

One agent said, "Don't call me every day, but if you send me a press kit on Monday, call me on Friday, and if we don't connect, try again on the following Tuesday. Twice a day is a nuisance, every day can be too much, but you just don't want to disappear either. Come up with different reasons to call: maybe a new CD, new promo material, or a new list of places you might be playing."

Agents and club owners who don't call back are a fact of life.

Some do. Many don't. The booking contact for Juanita's Cantina in Little Rock, Arkansas, says, "I tell people to be a thorn in my side. Call me so I get to know your voice and your name. Be persistent, but be professional."

Many times when you try to make contact with a booking agent, or anyone who can make a decision about using your group, you will get voice mail or an answering machine. Some of these people get 150 messages a day and can't possibly return them all. Either that, or they're very selective. Put yourself in their shoes. Which one of these messages would you return?

1) This is Bill Jackson. Please give me a call back at 555-1234.

2) Hi Mike, this is Bill Jackson. I heard you book bands.

Be persistent but be very professional. Call me back at 555-1234.

3) Hi Mike, this is Bill Jackson. My group is The Fun Seekers and I've got some great news for you if you'd like to give me a call. My cell phone is 555-1234.

4) Hi Mike. This is Bill Jackson. Your friend Wayne Baker asked me to give you a call. We've got a group that I think would be perfect for your club. I'd like to send you a promo kit and CD. If you don't think we'd fit, I won't waste your time. Please give me a call with an address to send it to. My cell phone is 555-1234 and I have it on most of the time.

5) Hi Mike. This is Bill Jackson. Our group just finished five weeks at the Sterling Nugget and we've got a good following. I think we might be a fit for your club and I'd appreciate a chance to discuss it with you, but first I'd like to send you a couple of our CDs and promo kits, plus a recent poster if you have any interest. You can reach me at 555-1234 or on my cell at 555-2244. Please let me know. I won't waste your time if you have no interest. Thanks.

Which of these calls would you return? Bet number 1 or 2 wouldn't get to the top of your priority list on a busy day. But the messages do get stronger as you go down the list. If your message is similar to number 4 or 5 and you don't hear back, wait a day or two and try again. You might then say you don't want to waste their time or yours, but you would appreciate a call. And each time you leave a message, say something else that is new or positive about your group. Mention upcoming radio airplay, or offer to send a video from your last gig. But don't send expensive promo material blind. Find out if they're the right person to send it to. You also want to find out a little more about their club, and that's going to take a return call.

Also, if you do get a return call, and they're not interested at the moment because they don't book more than ten weeks out, think you're too expensive, think you need more experience, or don't have time to talk with you, don't give up. Keep them on your list. Give them a call or send them a note once in a while. Things change. The more people you talk to on a regular basis, the more work you're going to get. It's the stay-in-their-face rule of keeping your calendar full.

Are Your Business Cards Helping You Get More Gigs?

You can be a great talent, but sometimes it takes a little more than playing ability to get those decent-paying gigs. You also have to have some marketing smarts to keep yourself booked. Even if your potential clients have seen you perform, they still need something to hold in their hand that tells them how to reach you when they want to book you. A name and phone number on the back of a bar napkin doesn't quite make it. You want to stand out from all the other groups and musicians in your area, and that begins with the very basics—those little billboards you carry in your pocket or purse. It starts with your business card.

Make your card a good reflection of who you are. How do you use your business cards? Think about it. Do you have them at all? Do they sit idly in a box at home, only to be tossed out when your area code changes? Or do they come out of your pocket as soon as someone asks, "How do I contact you to book you?" Do you find that they're great for picking your teeth? Do you write notes to yourself on the back? Or do they help you find more playing gigs or create more repeat bookings?

Check your business cards. Are they current? Do they have all the up-to-date information on how to reach you? Do your cards include your home phone number, your cell phone number, and your e-mail address? Do they have information about your Web site, if you have one? Are they a good representation of you or your band? When you give out a card, does it look brand new, or does it look like it's been used once or twice before?

An e-mail address on a business card shows that you're keeping up with the times. Listing day and evening phone numbers, maybe a pager or a cell phone number, shows that you're very accessible. And a card that isn't stained or dog-eared shows that you are concerned with quality and appearance. How about the backs of your business cards? Is this space used at all? Maybe you could list names of the better places you've played, or current CDs you have available.

There can be a lot of information and a ton of phone numbers. Don't make the mistake of trying to cram it all onto one side. That's why the fold-over card with three to four sides of usable space is a good option. One rule of thumb is to make sure that you can put a quarter somewhere on your business card without covering text. If there isn't enough blank space to set a quarter on it anywhere, you may be overdoing it. So before you add your band's name and the number of years you've been playing together; everybody's phone, fax, pager, cell numbers; the titles of all your CDs; and the famous names you've worked with, think about image. Think about the possibility of confusing a potential client, and whether your business card will stand out.

But that's just the beginning. How you use them is as important as the look of the cards themselves. Some musicians take their cards to another level. And so do the DJs. Check it out if you want to compete in the same arena.

You can have different cards for different uses. Maybe you want a double-sided card with a perforated half for requests. Or you may have a special card just for fans, or to leave with a tip in a restaurant on which you can simply write "thanks." Now you have someone who could possibly pass your name on for potential work when the topic comes up.

This does not mean that you have to spend thousands of dollars on business cards. Some of the most creative forms require little or no money. In fact, there's a musician in the Midwest who seldom gives out his regular card. When a customer says, "Man, what are you doing playing in this place? Let me have your name and phone number—my friend's a concert promoter," he goes to his wallet, pulls out a blank check and rips it in half so just his name, address, and phone numbers are on it. He writes a little note on the bottom and says, "Use this." Then, even after four scotches, his customer will remember him when he empties his pocket, even if there are six other business cards mixed in. (There's no business like show business.)

If your card is no different than those of your local landscaper or cleaner, you might want to rethink the whole process.

There's a musician in New York who says he doesn't like to have business cards that are the same shape and size as everyone else's. So when someone asks for his card, he merely takes out a three-by-five-inch index card and writes his name, address, and phone number on it very neatly with a felt-tip pen. He says that it really stands out from the little stack of regular business cards the person has been accumulating from other area bands. It's certainly a lot bigger, doesn't get lost, and has a personal touch. And then he writes, "If you're serious, I'll send you a press kit and a CD!" It's a great hook.

If your business cards are no different from those of your local landscaper, painter, or septic-tank cleaner, you might want to rethink the whole process. You might want to take a long look at what it would take to make your cards a better reflection of yourself and your band.

Business cards can help to bring in gigs; they're great for referrals; and they can be one of the best methods of personal advertising you have. Take a look at some of the business cards you have collected yourself. If your business card doesn't match their uniqueness and go beyond their creativity, now's the time to do something about it. It's Marketing 101.

By the way, I wrote a complete book on this subject called *Here's My Card* (Renaissance Books, 2000). It's in bookstores and on www.amazon.com if you want to check it out. *Here's My Card* gives dozens of ideas on how to use something as simple as your business card to get more work.

Competing for Gigs
with Mobile DJs

Nothing is worse than losing a gig to a mobile DJ. You take music lessons, spend thousands and thousands of dollars, practice for years to become a professional musician, then someone right out of high school buys a few CDs, gets some sound equipment, and starts stealing jobs right out from under you. Those gigs they're grabbing include weddings, corporate events, private parties, and school dances. Take a look in the yellow pages of your local phone book and you'll find more of them than you do bands and orchestras. They're becoming more prevalent than pizza shops. They're replacing live music with one person playing recorded tunes on discount-store speaker systems for less money.

At least that's how it seems. The only trouble is that perception is not reality. My suggestion is to go to an event where one of the better mobile DJs is working. You could be in for a jolt. I've met these people. They are young and aggressive. You might find out that one-person CD show is charging more than a four-piece group. And he or she has enough equipment to fill up a good-sized U-Haul truck. Also, it might not be just one person. It could be a technician and an entertainer/host. Some use props and will dress to fit the occasion.

Before you think that those DJs are stealing the good gigs and working for next to nothing, do a little reality check. Some of these people are charging in the thousands. Find out how you can compete in areas they can't. You also have to compete in their areas of expertise. And to compete, you need to find out whom you're competing with. There are DJs and KJs. KJs are Karaoke Jocks who sing along with the CDs, entertain, and get the audience involved. Many DJs and KJs provide constant entertain-ment, cater to the audience, and have sophisticated lighting equipment. They bring along fog machines, bubble machines, and confetti guns; and they charge big bucks.

If you're going to compete in the big bucks for entertainment cat-egory, what can you bring to the party? What can you do that's really exciting, different, and creative? The DJ thing isn't as easy as you may think. Many DJs bring as much equipment as a band carting around a Hammond B-3, two Leslie speakers, several drum sets, six big guitar amps, and a complete sound system. It's a lot of stuff. And they play nonstop. They get the audience involved. How about you? When you take a break, is anything going on? You could easily tape your group as you play each set, then have the tape play through your sound sys-tem on the break. How about lights? It's not enough just to play well any more. You have to look spectacular for some of these events. And audience involvement? If you don't know what tunes are hot right now, you'd better learn quickly. Infiltrate their industry. Pick up one of the mobile DJ magazines. Find out how they involve the audience, and how they get their work. See what niches they go after. Find out where the better-known ones are working and go see their shtick.

Find out how to involve the audience— know what tunes are hot.

How about your promotional materials? Are your business cards and brochures up to date? Do you have them at all? How about a demo CD? Demo video? The DJs do...at least the ones that get a lot of work. Do you have an 800 number, a Web site, and an e-mail address? Are you in the yellow pages under "entertainment" as well as "bands and orchestras"? Do you have a particular niche where you can excel as a band, an orchestra, or a single? And as a professional musician, you stand out as being serious about your work.

Most people would rather hear live musicians than a recording. Most people would rather hear live musicians than a recording. That's in your favor right away. For dancing, most people prefer a band to a CD. Take advantage of it. Promote yourself and your group in ways that DJs can't. "Live music is best" is not just a slogan. It's true. Many people think DJs are cheaper than a band. They're not, at least not all of them. And even if they are, your talent and everything else you can bring to the party can run rings around the CD spinners. When you can compete on the entertainment side as well as talent, your bookings could increase dramatically.

Dialing for Gigs

When you're looking for work and trying to fill your calendar, one of the easiest methods is to use the phone. I know what you're thinking: "Cold calling on the phone to find work...yuck." Rejection. Frustration. Most people would rather go to the dentist than call people they don't know. Maybe you think it's beneath you as a professional musician. Few people like to put themselves in the same category as those who call during dinner to solicit changing your long distance service. But hang on. It doesn't have to be that way at all. Using the phone to find decent-paying gigs can be a good way to keep your calendar filled. It works if you do it right. If you're not seeing results, you're doing it wrong.

First of all, unless the club owner, talent buyer, or check writer knows you or has heard you, it's going to be very difficult to get a booking over the phone. And it's impossible to get them to sign a contract on the phone. So the best you can do is establish a little interest and create some rapport. Get the name of the person who might do the booking, and arrange to get him or her to hear you. If he or she can't hear you live, send a demo CD and/or a promotional kit.

Think of calling for work on the phone as the same way a cruise ship docks. Have you ever watched a big ship tie up? When it nestles up to the dock, a huge rope isn't flung overboard. A deck hand throws out something that looks like a tennis ball connected to heavy-duty fishing line. That line is connected to heavier rope, which is then connected to a line used to tie up the ship. If you tossed the heavy rope overboard first, you'd either miss the dock or kill somebody. It's the same thing with dialing for dollars.

You don't spill everything you have all at once. Your first priority should be to determine if there is any chance for you to take the contact to the next level. If you call a club and find out that they pay less than you want even if you just opened for Bruce Springsteen (or *are* Bruce Springsteen), then you've just saved yourself the trouble of going there in person. If they pay decent money, and you can convince them that you are terrific and worth listening to—either in person or on CD—you then have a good shot at booking the gig. To do this effectively, you might have to take your phone skills up a notch, and use some decent business chops.

Create some interest in yourself or your group. You can do this in less than three minutes on the phone. Find out whom you're speaking to, let them know who you are, find out if you're the type of band or single they use, get them to like you over the phone,

Your main purpose should be to take that contact to the next level.

and tell them you're really good at what you do. You're worth a listen. You're worth a look. Find out what dates they might consider booking you if your demo CD/press kit knocks them out of their chairs. Don't go overboard on the phone. If you've played Vegas, New York clubs, or headlined some major jazz venues, you can slip that in on the phone. If you've worked cruise ships or Letterman, tell them that, too. But if you haven't done anything more significant than an occasional wedding at the VFW hall, don't let them know you're just getting into the mainstream. Let the buyer decide how good you are after they hear or see you.

One great way to get gigs over the phone is to mention that one of their friends or peers suggested you give them a call. Use a name they might know. Of course, you want to ask that person if you can use him or her as a reference first. And if the club owner, talent buyer, or check writer asks what you have coming up and your gig calendar is sparse, don't tell them you have nothing booked. Tell them you've got some private gigs (which could be practice sessions in your living room) or out-of-town dates (you could be taking your kids to Disney), but could check your calendar to see if anything matches the date(s) they have open. Sound busy, but don't make something up if you can't back it up. You want to appear to be working. You don't want to sound like you're calling with a tin cup in your hand.

Make cold calls with the intent of building up your database.

If your prospect is interested in you or your group and wants demo info, always ask permission to call again after they receive it. Try to set a specific date for calling back. Then, when you call, you can start the conversation with, "You asked me to give you a call back today." That makes it sound as if the call was their idea.

Make cold calls with the purpose of building up your database for gigs. The more viable names and phone numbers with pertinent information you have on your database, the more work you'll get. Keep in touch with these people. Find out who else they know who might be able to book you. Keep the calls friendly, short, and to the point. Following up on leads is critical at this point. If you keep in touch, put them on your mailing list, let them know where you are playing, and send them up-to-date promotional material, you could very easily see your calendar filled to capacity.

Creating an Endless Stream of Bookings

I have a golfing buddy who also plays trumpet. He told me that bookings were starting to get a little soft. I asked him why. He said he figured it had to do with a lot of things.

1) There's no work in this town anymore.

2) The economy is in the dumpster.

3) Things haven't recovered from 9/11.

4) People are buried in debt and can't get out.

5) The stock market has to shake out before things get any better.

6) The corporate gigs don't exist anymore.

7) We're in a recession.

8) Mobile DJs are getting all the work.

9) He only wants to play Dixie or cool jazz and nobody wants that type of band around here.

10) The only music that sells is rock.

Wow. If making excuses was an Olympic event, this guy could be a gold-medal contender. I asked him exactly what he was doing to try to turn things around. He said he was out of ideas. The phone doesn't ring anymore like it used to. The clubs that booked his band aren't using groups like his right now. So then I asked him if he thought about asking for referrals, or following up on past contacts. He said he didn't like to ask for referrals. Doesn't want to impose on people. And therein lies the problem. He "doesn't want to." Asking for and following up referrals won't work if you don't want it to work.

> **Asking for referrals won't work if you don't really want it to.**

Referrals are a great source of more gigs. But the problem is we don't think about it when playing a club date, wedding, or corporate gig. The first thing we usually think about when getting a contract signed is how much we're getting paid. And then we worry that the check won't clear. We don't say, "By the way, we get a lot of new bookings from people like yourself who like our group. Do you know someone who might use a group like ours?"

Asking for a referral is step one. You have to ask, and you have to use a little personality at the same time. Believe it or not, most of the time you will get a name. Sometimes two. Then just let it go. Sometimes people will give you a name either to help you out, or to get out of the conversation. Don't start with, "I'll give you a cut if they book us." That puts them in an awkward position. Friends help out their friends. If you have made them a friend, it's easy to ask for the name of a referral.

Step two is a little different. You have to follow up on the referral. That's tougher. It's almost like a cold call. But if you really want more gigs, you simply have to do it. Just pick up the phone and call. If you get an answering machine, just leave your name, phone number and a message that you've got "good news" for them. Nothing more. People love good news. They will probably return your call. When you finally get a chance to speak to them, mention **Try to get them to hear you play, or meet you personally.** the person who referred you. Explain you are just doing your job. It's how you earn your living. Be nice. Joke with them. Get them to be your friend. Try to get some positive acceptance or just try to get them to hear your band or meet you personally.

There's a very good chance that if they have even the remotest amount of interest they'll come in to hear you or would be willing to meet with you. If they don't, and you have established some rapport with them over the phone, ask them if they know somebody who would be interested in using your group. Tell them again that you're just doing your job. It's how you make a living, and you appreciate anything they can do to help. Again, niceness pays off.

Asking for referrals is a skill. You have to ask at the right time. Ask when they are the most excited, either after they sign the contract, or after you play the gig and everybody is happy. Also, don't forget about networking with your musician buddies. Let them know you're looking for gigs. Maybe they can use you on an upcoming gig. Maybe they know of someone who is looking for a group on a date they can't fill. Brainstorm on getting work, and remember there is strength in numbers. Don't be afraid to ask where you might be able to find the next gig, or who could refer you. Referrals are the major source of new leads.

Referrals are a major source of new leads.

If they say that they don't know anybody, don't belabor it. You tried. Let them think about it. They might even call you back in a day or two with a name. Or a month later they may mention your name in a conversation, say you played a great gig, and suggest someone call you. It just takes that first step of letting them know that referrals are an important part of your business. That's how you get more gigs. Referrals could provide you with an endless stream of contacts that will get you through the slow periods.

What Are You Doing Today to Help Your Career Tomorrow?

I found an interesting book that is out of print, in a secondhand bookstore. It's called *You Can't Afford the Luxury of a Negative Thought*, by Peter McWilliams (Prelude Press, 1997). Even though it was written for the general public, it really makes sense for musicians. Anyone who's ever had an instrument in his hands and gone out and played it for money knows what I'm talking about. Negative words, statements, and thoughts can run rampant in the music business. They can kill a career. They can destroy dreams.

They come from club owners:
"Are you crazy charging that much?"
"Your sound will never bring in a crowd."
From friends and loved ones:
"Get yourself a real job."
"Playing music is not a living."
From other musicians:
"There's no work around here."
"You'll never make it big."
And how many times have you said to yourself:
"I just don't get the breaks."
"Other musicians get all the work."
"If I only had a better instrument."

I was sitting in a bar listening to a great group a couple of weeks ago. The keyboard player came and sat with me during one of the breaks. Here's what he said: "Everyone tells me I'm the best in the area, but the phone doesn't ring." And, "I can't stand working with these guys." Then, "No one wants to pay anything decent in this town."

When he told me that he had great equipment and could play as good as any major name in the business, but couldn't get any work, I turned to him and said, "So, exactly what are you doing about it?" He said, "Huh?" I said, "What are you doing to turn things around for yourself?" He said, "There's nothing that I can do." So I said, "Okay, it's over. You believe it, I'm convinced, maybe you can sell cars. Update your resume. Look into multi-level marketing. Deliver pizzas. Give it up."

Don't let the "can'ts," "won'ts," and "nevers" start to monopolize your thinking.

Well, that knocked him back a couple of steps. While he was stammering, thinking about what to say next, I asked him what his dream gig would be. He said, "Playing Las Vegas, backing up major shows." I asked him if that's what he really wanted to do, then whom has he contacted, did he talk to any musicians in Las Vegas, did he think about moving, did he network with any casinos or clubs out there? He said, "No, it would never work; I couldn't do it." So I said, "Then don't tell me you can't, tell me you don't want to."

And therein lies the truth. We become prophets of our own destiny when all the "can'ts," "won'ts," and "nevers" start to monopolize our brains.

Here are a few tips from one of the chapters in that book. "Hang around people who have a positive direction in their life. They are rewarding to be around. Hanging around people who are addicted to negative thinking can be a drag. They feed you negativity and criticize every positive move you make." If this describes anyone in your band, you might want to assess if they are holding you and your career back. Fill your life with people who applaud your positive thoughts, feelings, and actions. Surround yourself with people who encourage you toward better things and achieving your goals. Don't let negative thinking sabotage your dreams and plans.

When things start to go in the dumpster, when the gigs aren't coming in, when the money isn't as good as you want, you have two choices:

1) You can moan, whine, complain, and tell everybody how bad things are.

2) You can do something about it.

If you select option number one, you might consider packing up your horn, keyboard, guitar, or drums and getting out of the music business. If you select the second, you can start by finding some uplifting people to talk to. Do some things you haven't done before to bring excitement into your life. This doesn't mean going to a Dale Carnegie class and shouting, "I've got enthusiasm!" It does mean stepping back and taking a good look at what you can do to make your music career go in the direction you want. It might mean moving. It might mean finding a different niche. It might mean doing some serious marketing. It might mean finding another group of musicians to hang around with. It might mean a serious attitude change.

Surround yourself with people who encourage you to achieve your goals.

It doesn't mean griping to the world about it. You see, if you do what you have always done, you will get what you have always gotten. Nothing will change. And you will drag everybody down at the same time. One thing about telling people your problems is that 80 percent of the people don't care, and the other 20 percent are actually glad you have them.

The best thing is to take a step back, come up with a game plan to make things better, and work a little harder at taking your music career to another level. Good things will happen. It does take a little luck, but the harder you work, the luckier you will get. So get that new CD out. Update your press kit. Add to your mailing list. Nothing can hold you back. You can do it, if that's what you really want. Good luck.

Chapter 4

MONEY

FOUR

Are You Getting
What You're Worth?

How much do you get for a gig? How do you set your rates? If you're a band, do you price yourself at what everybody else is getting, just to be competitive? If you're a single, are you working to pay the bills, playing to have some fun and make a few bucks on the weekend, or playing to get yourself to a better level of money and gigs? You know how much your playing is worth. You decide for yourself.

Earning a living by playing an instrument is unlike any other profession. It's a great business. It can generate a lot of revenue. And it's a lot of fun. If you want to do something that's not fun, you could sell insurance, I suppose. I don't know a whole lot of insurance salespeople who read policies for fun.

I recently talked to a piano player from Connecticut who gets a lot of work playing private parties in the area, including Manhattan and Long Island. She doesn't do club gigs. She tries to go where the money is by playing corporate events and private functions.

Decide what you are worth —don't let your customer do it for you. She said she had to play a lot of "crap gigs" just to get her name around. But she likened it to being a plumber, painter, or mechanic. She said that you have to get your name out there, you have to stay in their faces, and you have to get people to notice you. Another interesting thing she said was, "If you charge more, people will respect you. They may not always book you, but they will respect you and they'll tell their friends about you. One gig at a decent fee makes up for three or four at a lower price." Decide what you're worth. Don't let your customer do it for you.

There was a great book out a number of years ago called *How to Sell More Cookies, Condos, Cadillacs, Computers...and Everything Else* (Random House, 1986). It was written by a 12-year-old Girl Scout named Makita Andrews who sold more Girl Scout cookies than anybody else in the country. Her secret was pretty simple, "You have to go where the money is." She also advised, "You have to talk to a lot of people." Some people buy, some people don't. She didn't discount the cookies; you don't have to discount the price you charge to play. But if a club can get all the bands they want without paying a lot, you probably aren't going to get really big bucks from them unless you're as much in demand as the Dixie Chicks. If club owners think you're worth the money, you'll get it. If they don't, you won't.

I have a friend who is in a band that plays weddings, private parties, country clubs, etc. They have one price. It's about double what most other bands in the area charge for the same kind of gig, but they stick to their price. Each year they get more work. They come up with reasons customers should pay more: better entertainment, better sound system, better vocals, creative audience participation, lighting, continuous music, fog, current tunes, current dances. My friend says, "I have no problem with bands that charge less—they know what they're worth."

So the bottom line is: to get better work, more money, and more gigs, you have to go where they can pay better and where they think you're worth the money. You might have to improve the quality of your playing and find ways to be more entertaining at the same time. The only one who knows how much you're worth is you. It's not the club, the client, or the customer. Set your price. Figure out what it's going to take, and then come up with your own plan for how to get it.

Getting Bigger Bucks Means Asking for Bigger Bucks

Price is a delicate subject with musicians. As professionals, we want to make a decent wage, without overpricing ourselves and losing a gig. It's a fine line to walk. It's always disheartening when another group yanks a job away from us because they're charging a ridiculously small amount of money. But I guess they know what their music is worth.

What if your neighbor said he was going to have a heart bypass operation and found a doctor who would do the whole procedure for $500? How good would you think the doctor was? Or a mechanic who says he can replace your car's engine for only $200, including labor? Do you think that engine would actually run? Now how about musicians who are willing to work for next to nothing?

I had an interesting conversation with a person involved in the music industry in California. I told him that I believed that professional musicians should get paid according to their talent. He told me I didn't understand the music business out there. Bands don't get paid. They pay to play. Or they play for free, sell tickets, and get the proceeds from the door.

This person was not a musician himself, but he is heavily involved in the music industry. His perception was that "finding gigs that pay big bucks" is not possible for aspiring musicians. Not in California anyway.

I attempted to set him straight. I know there are a lot of west-coast musicians who do well. All of a sudden, I found myself a committee of one trying to widen his tunnel vision. And this guy is surrounded by musicians. The problem is that he knows so many musicians who give their services away, he thinks that it's the norm rather than the exception.

Ask for what you think you're worth. Raise your self-esteem a couple of notches. Being a professional musician means getting paid like one. I don't care if you play at weddings, corporate gigs, rock concerts, or local clubs. If you don't ask for a decent price, you will never get it. And you don't know if you are going to get it until you ask.

If you don't ask for a decent price, you will never get it.

It begins with your own perception of your musical worth. I have a friend who plays piano in a small town. I asked him how much he gets a night, and he told me it is just union scale, nothing more. He plays well. I asked why he doesn't charge more. He said, "Nobody would pay it." I asked him if he ever asked for more. Had he ever lost any gigs because his price was too high? He said no, he never tried. I think if he asked for triple his fee and got it, he wouldn't know what to do.

If you've got a decent demo CD, a professional video showing you or your group in action, a good-looking press kit, great credentials, and super references, then price yourself accordingly. And that's the catch. If you don't have any of the above, then you're back to square one.

So, instead of going back to the woodshed and honing your chops in the hopes of cranking more cash, maybe you should work on your support materials. You want people who pay well to come knocking on your door. But first you have to let them know where your door is. And you have to let them know they can't get in for free, or for anything less than you think you're worth. If you don't think you're worth more, guess what? You're not. People are not going to say, "That's all you want? Here, let me pay you more."

I know someone who plays guitar, sings, and puts on a really great show at a variety of venues. He says if he doesn't lose at least one job a month because of price, he's not charging enough. But the jobs he does get pay very well. It's that old adage: the squeaky wheel gets the grease.

We need to charge a decent buck. Most importantly, we need to educate the musicians who are playing for next to nothing, and explain to them that there's another world out there. It starts by spreading the word yourself. Many musicians don't know what to charge or how to charge. Maybe you can be a one-person committee to help change their thinking, one musician at a time.

If you've got a serious electrical problem in your house, you know that professional electricians have a lot of experience and know what they're doing; you're not going to get jolted

Let them know they're getting talent that they can count on.

into the next county when you throw a light switch. As a professional musician, you can let people know they're going to get talent they can count on for whatever playing job they have. They know they will pay accordingly, just like they pay the best carpenter or plumber. Sometimes you just have to ask. Don't let your own tunnel vision get in the way.

Go Where
the Money Is

There's no end to the ways you can make money playing a musical instrument. Getting bigger bucks is a little more tricky. You're a professional musician. You spent a long time learning your trade. Your paycheck for playing should reflect your qualifications. When somebody calls you, many times they've already decided to book you. They probably have an idea of what you charge and it's just a matter of date and time and if your calendar's open. But going out to get work—better paying work—can be a hassle, a grind, and, occasionally, a lesson in facing rejection. However, if you want to expand your horizons beyond local bars, weddings at the American Legion, or the people who say, "You charge HOW MUCH?" then you might want to think about going where the money is.

You know how it goes. You try to get a gig at a local club that uses live music on the weekends. The next thing you hear is, "Your price is too high." Okay, they're entitled to their opinions. But what if they're right? Maybe your price is too high for that joint. Maybe they're used to having bands play for next to nothing, play for exposure, or for whatever they can take in at the door. Maybe they can only afford so much because of the size of the place, their overhead, or their cash constraints. So, if you want work that actually spins off decent revenue, this is probably not the place for you. There are a lot of places to get work if you don't let your ego stand in your way.

There are a lot of places to get work if you don't let your ego stand in your way.

There's a pianist in Long Island whose niche is in playing private parties. She goes after people who have expensive homes, hold regular social functions, and own horses. In fact, she plays a lot of parties before and after horse shows. She says that these people are used to spending large amounts of money for entertaining, so when she quotes her substantial fee they don't flinch.

If you're set on getting decent money at your local clubs, you had better come up with some reasons they should book you and pay your fee. You might have to think about marketing yourself better, and selling yourself differently. Maybe you have a new CD release that's starting to get airplay. Maybe you have your own mailing list of people who will come to hear you. Maybe you can offer to do the mailing for the club and absorb the cost yourself to insure that the place is packed. Of course, for this, you charge bigger bucks. When club owners know there will be wall-to-wall customers, the odds are in your favor of getting what you think you're worth.

Give them a good reason to book you and pay your fee.

Find out what some of the places you're thinking of playing have paid musicians and groups in the past. If you're looking for much more, chances are they'll pass on you or your group unless there's a tremendous benefit to them. And that benefit has to be in the cash register.

So if bigger bucks are what you're looking for, start looking where the bigger bucks are being paid. It's kind of common sense, but if they can't afford you, then you're spinning your wheels. Many private parties, charity functions, one-time social events, political programs, and major corporate events will pay very well. You just have to search them out, sell yourself, and ask for the money.

To do this you'd better look pretty slick on paper too. That includes a well-put-together promo kit, great business cards, a decent demo video and/or CD, current press releases, significant references, local and regional endorsements, and color as well as black-and-white promotional pictures. You want to let people know where you've played, where you will be playing, and a few positive comments from people, clubs, and organizations who have booked you in the past. Then the money starts to flow. One good gig will get you two more. The trick is to get the first one that pays really well to get the ball rolling. They're out there. You just have to figure out where to look.

You have to search out the bigger bucks and ask for the money.

Know the
Wedding Planner

I read a newspaper article on the price of weddings. It was an interesting, well-researched item on how young couples (or their parents) spend their money to make the big day memorable. It said that even a small wedding could run a bill of $20,000, and larger weddings could go through the roof. As an example, the article took one couple and listed their anticipated expenses for a September wedding. The grand total was $108,255. I looked it over very carefully and was astonished to see that one of the most minimal expenses was for music—and that was for a DJ. Five hundred dollars for a CD spinner, when the candy favors alone were $2,000! That's just crazy! What's wrong with this picture?

First of all, weddings are a great source of work for professional musicians. And that's not just for wedding bands playing cover songs like "Celebration," "Shout!" and "The Chicken Dance." That's also for pianists, harpists, string quartets, bagpipers, strolling accordian players, and the like. But these gigs don't just fall into your lap. You have to make yourself known. You have to get to know the wedding planners in your area; you need to schmooze caterers, florists, limo companies, and photographers. You need to know what your role really is, you need to know how to work with the caterer, and you have to help coordinate the entire affair. Otherwise, the gig goes to a 20-year-old kid in a tuxedo, minus the jacket, who introduces the bride and groom, spins some tunes, and gets paid more than he can make at McDonald's. It's not right.

Let them know you are better than a kid with a turntable.

More and more people are using wedding planners today. That's one person who does all the work, is in on all the wedding decisions, and knows how to spend money... lots of it. Search them out. Let them know who you are, and that you are better than any kid with a turntable and a couple of speakers. Let them know you have formal wear, and you have lights, fog, confetti guns, and bubble machines, or will get them. You have (or can get) an expanded sound system if necessary. You can provide nonstop music, do the introductions, and work with the caterer, the videographer, and the bridal party. If you don't, can't, or won't—you simply can't compete.

You are a professional, a live entertainer —you're worth the money.

You are a professional, a live entertainer. You are the best. Of course the cost is going to be more than 500 bucks. But they're paying a thousand dollars just for flowers! They can pay a lot more than that for a great band that knows how to work the room for a wedding. You are worth the money. If you're not, it's back to the kid with the CDs who does four weddings a week and takes money out of your pocket.

Don't let them take this work away from you. Compete. Learn the business. Do what it takes. Don't think that it's just money because that's only an excuse for not getting the gig. Remember, DJs come with all the toys, nonstop music, and the whole wedding thing down pat. So if you can provide the same with live music—provide music during the breaks, do the intros, coordinate the affair, schmooze the crowd, and work with the wedding party, they will pay. If you are really good, they will pay more. If you are GREAT, they will pay a lot more. It's like mining for gold. You have to go where it is first, and you need the right tools. It doesn't happen by accident.

Is Playing for "Exposure" Worth It?

We've all had these calls. The phone rings, and it's some club or commercial venue asking us to come down and play for "exposure." You know, they tell you tons of people will hear you, you can give out cards, you can get your name out there, etc. It's a myth. Don't fall for it. You're a professional musician. You've spent a lot of money and time on your craft. Don't put yourself in the category of someone who will play for free.

I know of a harpist who got a call from an upscale department store looking for entertainment during the Christmas holiday season. They were having a special sales event on a Sunday evening and they wanted her to play in their store for several hours. In lieu of payment, they said she could hand out her business cards and get "lots of exposure." Her comeback was great. She said, "I can't do that, but how about this? I will be playing for lots of fancy parties over the holidays. If you give me one of your special occasion dresses from the formalwear department, I will wear the dress and tell everyone that it came from your store. Your fashions will get lots of exposure." After a slight pause, the caller said, "I see your point."

I bet that if that store needed someone to fix the heating system or a plumber to fix a leak, they wouldn't call them and offer them exposure. Or if one of their clerks got hurt and they had to get emergency help, they wouldn't offer a doctor exposure in exchange for medical assistance. Why is it so commonplace to offer musicians visibility instead of payment?

One of the reasons is that too many bands and musicians will do it, and that sets a bad precedent for other musicians. There are musicians and bands that will play for any audience without compensation as long as they feel they are the star(s) of the show. They will work for nothing, or practically nothing, at a club where they really want to play. And as long as there are musicians who will do this (or in some cases PAY to play a club so they can work for the door), we will continue to be asked to pro-vide entertainment for free.

There are more drawbacks in playing for free than there are benefits.

Certainly there are times when you can do something for benefits or charities. But don't fall for the exposure myth because there are more drawbacks in playing for free than there are any possible benefits. You'll quickly learn that you'll have an immediate reputation as someone who will play for free. One free gig will probably get you another freebie call, and that can lead you down the road to starvation. Consistently playing for a decent fee prevents you from getting that reputation.

The public also tends to think that musicians don't really work, they're doing something for fun. Perhaps part of the blame lies with the word that musicians themselves use when referring to what they do: "play." It's possible that when members of the pub-lic hears us use this word, they associate it with fun, rather than work. And if we are having fun, they think, why should we get paid too?

It's important to remember—and to get audiences to remember—that while we certainly do enjoy making music, we are also pro-fessionals, and we do this to make money so that we can pay bills and support our families. Try getting Tiger Woods or David Duvall to appear for free at your local golf course or country club. They don't play golf just for the fun of it. It's their living.

Perception is important, and as professional musicians, it is important not to let our talent and integrity slide. Would you go to a heart specialist who was doing operations at discount prices? People have a higher regard for things that cost them money. They will treat you with more respect when they have to pay, and I bet the more you charge, the more respect you get.

People have a higher regard for things that cost them more money.

People want to get what they pay for. And they want it worth what they have to pay.

There are a lot of ways to get around a freebie request, maintain dignity, and still get the job. Maybe the person who called you really wanted to book you, but was just testing the waters. Maybe they actually had a budget, but just wanted to see if you would play for free. If you explain nicely that you are a professional, possibly they might come up with the money, or find someone who will. Instead of hitting them with a direct no, try asking if they can find a sponsor.

Explain that you can't play for free, but you will give them the opportunity to find the money someplace. If it's a corporate venue (like a store or major company), ask if they could get money from some other department, like advertising, marketing, or public relations. Act as if you have their best interests at heart, but you must have your best interests at heart as well.

Remember, musicians who work for free know what their time and talent is worth. The harpist had a great way of putting it, "Let's recognize the concept of playing for exposure for what it is…a myth." Exposure alone isn't worth it—you can die of exposure.

Chapter 5

DIVERSIFYING

One Good Wedding
Gig Can Get You Two More

You might not think there's a lot of repeat business from wedding gigs. Couples don't usually tell you they're going to do it again next month and ask if you have the date open. So what happens, more often than not, is you play the job, you get paid, and that's the last you hear from the happy couple. And even if they split up two years down the road, chances are they'll have a much smaller wedding the second or third time around. They'll probably skip the music and have a cookout in the backyard.

Wedding gigs can, however, generate referrals. After the wedding, you want to make sure you thank the couple and the parents of the bride and groom. Ask them if they were pleased, and before you load the last keyboard or amp into your van, ask them if any of their friends might be getting married in the near future.

It's basic. But many times we get the check and are more concerned about it clearing the bank than we are of future business. After the wedding you could send a personal thank-you note to the newly married couple with some of your business cards. Then, a few months later you could send a brochure on yourself or your group as a reminder that you do corporate work, class reunions, private parties, and whatever events you fit into.

Next year, send the couple an anniversary card. Put in a few more business cards. They'll be happy you thought of them and might refer you to somebody else who is getting married.

In fact, you might call them, chat with them as a friend, and ask them if they know somebody who might be able to use you or your group for their wedding. This is where brochures and demo CDs really help. A demo video of you or your group playing an actual wedding can make the difference in who gets chosen to play the gig. Very possibly they'll pass it along to someone they know who is getting married in the near future.

You want to make sure that everyone at the wedding knows the name of your band, and how to reach you if they want you to play another wedding or other type of gig. The problem is, you don't want blatant advertising to over-shadow an expensive party. You want to come across as a class act; no eight-sheet billboard draped in back of your group, or fly-ers that end up on the floor.

> **Make sure everyone there knows the name of your band and how to reach you.**

This is where request cards really play an important role. Have them printed as table tents, and perforated so your name and phone number are on the half they can keep. Keep them small and tasteful. Ask if you can put them on every table. If people bring the entire card up to you, simply tear off the request part and give them the other half "for a souvenir."

Most people won't write a request down or take the cards home. But they will look at them to see what's on them, and they'll find your name, the name of your group, and your phone number. You can use them again at your next wedding gig.

If the people at your wedding job don't know who you are, there is little chance they will search you out to book you or refer you. You want to make sure they know how to reach you when the subject of a band comes up. You need the creative business cards, the classy brochures, the informative flyers. Your materials have to be as professional as you are because they're reflections on you and your group. And you need to ask for referrals and leads.

Then it's up to you to follow them up. It's basic. It's necessary. It keeps the jobs coming in. Of course talent helps, but one without the other makes finding new jobs a little tough.

College Gigs

From August until May, universities and colleges are in full swing, so there's a good deal of work out there. Go after it! Fraternities and sororities are booking bands, doing house parties, and having their own tamed-down versions of "Animal House." Schools book groups for a variety of venues. A lot of school events are held outdoors, or in cafeterias or multipurpose rooms. Your competition might not be just other bands, but also comics, DJs, portable bungee jumping, and inflatable obstacle courses. There seems to be no limit to what colleges and fraternity/sorority houses will write a check for.

To go after these gigs, make a list of the schools in your area where you might want to play, and research them. Call the main office and ask who handles the bookings for college events. They'll also give you a list of their fraternities and sororities. This is where a little networking will go a long way. Find out the name of the entertainment director for each organization. Getting to know these people on a first-name basis will generate a raft of referrals, since these people know who does the same job in other fraternities/sororities. If nothing else, you will know that you're getting your press kit and demo material into the right hands.

You want to make sure that you keep a record of each conversation, so when you call back you'll know what the last discussion was about. Also, if you've already played a lot of successful college gigs (particularly at the same house over the years), use this to your advantage. You want the booker/check writer to know you'll make their job very easy by handling all the details, ensuring the gig goes off without a hitch, and making them look like a million bucks.

Remember, the person who booked you one year might not be around the next. That's where keeping in touch is essential. They can make it easier for you with their replacement by saying, "These guys are great—use them." Working fraternities and sororities is like playing a bar gig with a different manager/owner every year. Sometimes you have to start from scratch and sell yourself all over again.

On-campus college-supported activities are a completely different thing. Probably the majority of bands are booked through agents, but there are nonetheless a number of groups who represent themselves, and have good success with it. That's where the National Association for Campus Activities (NACA) comes in. NACA is an association of colleges and universities, and their members look to them to seek out entertainment acts. They have an extensive mailing list and programs on how to book bands and negotiate contracts. They can give you information regarding college bookings, as well as a list of agents who handle campus activities. If you want to work with an agent, NACA will give you information or help on getting one. NACA's phone number is (803) 732-6222, and their Web site is at www.naca.org.

The NACA can give you more information on college bookings.

Don't try to enlist an agent without first having a good press kit, sharp photos, references, a demo CD or video, and, most importantly, a group that fits in with the college crowd. This is one arena where "fake it 'til you make it" won't work, and you'll be nailed instantly. If your band has success at one venue, you'll reap

126

the benefits for months or years to come. But those repeat gigs won't happen unless you network constantly. It's not just a matter of who you know, it's who you know that can book you this semester. Students graduate; they drop out; they move on. College administrators change. Remember, this is not a bar gig. You are not going to be judged by how much money is rung up at the end of the night. You'll be judged by how well you fit, and how well you are liked. College and fraternity/sorority gigs are not the easiest jobs. Drinks spill, attitudes arise, and musical differences abound. But if you're wired for it, they can keep your calendar full and produce good revenue at the same time.

Corporate Gigs:
Nice Work If You Can Get It

I've always thought that corporate gigs were very different from club dates, weddings, and private parties. Playing for a large company is unique because you have to come up with an idea for the musical venue. Because this takes a little thought, many musicians shy away from these gigs. This just means less competition for you. Corporate gigs have a big payoff—not only can you charge more than for a regular gig, but you get paid with a secure check at the end of the night.

I remember learning that a Magicians' Convention was coming to our area. I found out the name of the program chairman and called him about playing for the event. He told me that most magicians play recorded music during their routine. I told him that while that might be true, magicians still need some music to bring them on and off the stage, and I could help coordinate this part of the program. For the magicians who just use waltz backgrounds, I could do it live and even put in the appropriate "stings." I ended up getting the job, did a few follow-up conventions, and enjoyed finding out how magicians make animals disappear and human bodies levitate. I also enjoyed my big paycheck. I would not have gotten the job if I had waited for the phone to ring.

I would not have gotten the job if I had waited for the phone to ring.

I learned an important lesson about pricing while doing a job for a GM dealer meeting. A meeting planner for one of their divisions liked my idea for incorporating my music into their program. When she asked how much I was going to charge, I stumbled around thinking of what the right price would be. Before I could answer she said, "It had better be enough, or they won't think you're any good." To these corporate execs, quality means a big price tag. Remember—value is in the mind of the beholder, and to some people four or five times scale is not a lot. You decide what you're worth.

I had a conversation with one of my professional musician friends who plays in a Dixie group. I asked how work was, and if they were doing a lot of club dates during the summer. He told me they couldn't do a lot of weekend club dates because they were doing a lot of "golf gigs." I had no idea what he was talking about. Then he told me that earlier in the year he had played during a one-day member-guest event at a local country club. The whole job involved playing for two hours after the tournament finished, while the players were coming in the club house and having drinks at the bar. It worked out well, so he contacted other clubs in the area. Some of the clubs had these events once a month. Every Monday many of these clubs had tournaments for charity events. Things like the heart, lung, and kidney foundations, or corporate events for local auto dealers. He would call the event coordinator, suggest his group play afterwards to "add some pizzazz" to the event. With this strategy, the group got a lot of extra work all summer long.

If you can advise the client on things, you could become a well-paid vendor.

If you can come up with an interesting way for a corporation, organization, or association to use your talents, you'll find you can charge for your creative part of the program as well. If they just want a single or group to play during a cocktail program, they can call musicians in the yellow pages, and probably get away with paying scale. But if you show them you can help with the program; maybe emcee, coordinate, or help with the theme; rehearse if it is part of the general meeting; or advise them on where live music could be a great fit, you become another well-paid vendor. It takes some work, but the revenue you can generate is well worth the extra trouble.

If you're in a metropolitan market where there are larger hotels and a convention center, check to see what meetings are coming up. You will be surprised at what organizations book their programs there. You probably never even heard of some of these companies and associations. Even so, they have social functions and need entertainers. Many of them rely on booking agents and event coordinators, but they could be using you. Find out who these people are, or just go directly to the meeting planner. The worst they can do is put you off to someone else. The nice part about these jobs is that corporations hold the same event year after year. After a while, you'll get to know these people and they'll book you again. They might even start calling you for other things they have in the area. The other residual benefit is that they know other meeting planners and can refer you. You have to be proactive and ask, but this is great work if you can get it. And as the song goes, "you can get it if you try!"

Panning for Gold at Business Events

Many musicians don't realize how much work there is in corporate functions and business events. The best corporate events are the ones that involve national meetings, attracting people from all over the country. The association, industry, manufacturer, or company rents a major hotel or convention center and holds meetings, dinners, and parties during the course of the multi-day event. It could be a trade show, new product announcement, dealer gathering, or whatever. The "party" part is where you come in.

The deal could be for a band to play after an awards banquet. Maybe someone is looking for a single during a cocktail party, or a combo to back up a singer, or live music to accompany speakers walking on and off the stage. Maybe they want a single or group to be part of a new product demonstration or company presentation. It could be anything! You just have to exert yourself to find out when the next program is coming up, who the meeting planner is, and how you can contact them.

The best cities for working corporate events are the destination cities like New York, Orlando, Chicago, Las Vegas, New Orleans, Toronto, Los Angeles, Anaheim, San Diego, Nashville, Miami, Dallas, and San Antonio. These cities have conventions, trade shows, and meetings booked years in advance. And by calling the meeting places or speaking with someone involved in day-to-day operations of the convention centers or major hotels in these cities, you can get a clue as to what's coming up, as well as who to call.

However, these are not the only cities that hold corporate events. Almost every city of any size that has decent facilities has these events scheduled year-round. Cities like Cleveland, Portland, Seattle, Sacramento, Reno, Denver, Kansas City, and Omaha. You get the picture. If your city has a major hotel and a place that can hold a trade show or large meeting, you probably have a shot at getting corporate work. There's even a lot of work in smaller cities like Rochester, NY; South Bend, IN; and Fresno, CA. I'd almost bet it's no different in your town, or at least in a bigger town nearby.

Have a CD and brochure ready for them because they have probably never heard you perform.

If you're going to go after this work, you'd better have a first-rate brochure and CD, because chances are that they've never heard of you or seen you perform. They'll decide whether to hire you based on your demo piece. A professional video would also be great.

You never know what might tip the scales in your favor for getting the work. First, find out what the venue is, who the meeting planner is, and what they might be looking for. You know—find a need and fill it. Come up with some ideas for making the meeting planner a hero.

A few years back, the Buick division of General Motors held a dealer meeting in New Orleans. They wanted a Dixieland group to play while they showed the new cars. They could've had their pick of dozens, if not hundreds, of groups in the area. But they decided instrumentation was more important than talent. They wanted a Dixie band that had a brass bass, not acoustic or electronic, and a banjo player. They wanted it to *look* like a Dixie group. They also wanted a piano player who had a digital keyboard because they couldn't supply a piano. Those were their main criteria. I attended the meeting. The band wasn't great (the clarinet player couldn't handle the charts), but the client was happy. Sometimes talent alone won't get the gig.

Some major talents appear at these corporate functions. Tony Bennett, Ray Charles, Kenny Rogers, and the Basie, Miller, and Dorsey bands do them all the time. But these functions don't go only to the big names. They use plenty of singles, show groups, and bands that play local gigs. It just depends on the type of function and how they want to use the music.

You won't believe how many corporate events there are. Boat companies, insurance companies, motorcycle manufacturers, real estate conglomerates, widget manufacturers, retailers, and wholesalers hold them every week, every month, every year. They go on week in, week out, all over the country. Associations, corporations, and charity organizations hold every type of event you can think of in your city, and you might not be aware of them.

Start by getting to know somebody at your local convention center. Get to know a meeting planner or two at some of the larger local industries or manufacturing facilities. Introduce yourself to the catering or sales manager at the major hotels in town. Marriotts, Sheratons, Radissons, and Hyatts are a good start. Find out about upcoming meetings and who's holding the functions. Make yourself known. Get some great references. Show a little personality.

If you want to be successful, you have to go where the gold is.

Remember, this is not going to happen overnight. These meetings are planned months and years in advance. If you want to book some of these great gigs, plan on being in it for the long haul. Many of these corporate planners spend tens of thousands, if not hundreds of thousands on their meetings. They spend a ton on audio, staging, and lighting. They pay speakers thousands of dollars to talk for only an hour. Think of what they might pay you if you just asked. But they won't come to you. You have to go out and find them. One good corporate gig could equal one week of club dates. It's like panning for gold. To be successful, you have to go where the gold is.

Here's a Gig You May Never Have Considered

Imagine—no rowdy crowds, no drunken customers, no late nights, and no low pay. You get to travel, meet interesting people, and talk about music and instruments all day. And nobody is throwing off-the-wall requests at you either. You get paid on time, and the check always clears the bank.

If this all sounds too good to be true, it's not. Product trainers, clinicians, and instrument specialists who work for major musical instrument manufacturers do this week in and week out. It's an easy gig for a musician with good personality skills and serious instrument chops, and who doesn't mind a different city each day. These musicians/product specialists hold clinics at retail music stores to demonstrate how to get the most out of an instrument, and to talk about (as well as demonstrate) the specifics of an instrument's features and benefits. These musicians are helpful to the company's regional sales representatives. They also assist the store manager when a clinic or training session is being held.

Musicians hold clinics at retail music stores to demonstrate instrument features.

The nice part of this gig is that you can really expand your chops playing things you like, network yourself in another sector of the music business, and have something to fall back on when your gig calendar isn't booked full. You meet some great people along the way, and your frequent flier miles will add up too. Those plane rides to Fargo, Dubuque, and Fresno in September might get you a free trip to St. Thomas or Key West in February. There are some great perks, too, like rental cars, food expenses, and decent hotels. It can be nice work.

While this job is great for the musician, he or she can also help a lot of different people in this line of work. For the salespeople in a local music store, an instrument specialist shows how to demonstrate a particular instrument, and discusses the latest models and features to make it easy to sell. For the customers, a product specialist basically demonstrates the product and suggests to the customer, "If you buy this instrument you can play like me!" Okay, okay, you have to be able to sell yourself and sell the product, but you're used to that—you sell yourself every time you go onstage anyway. Maybe that instrument you're demonstrating for those die-hard musicians at a local music store isn't your first choice, but on this gig it sure better be. If you can handle that part, with a little street smarts and personality, you could do really well.

So, how do you get these gigs? They're available with almost every major guitar, drum, and digital keyboard manufacturer. I talked about this to executives at Yamaha and Roland. Both companies have full-time and part-time specialists. A Yamaha executive said, "We want trainer-merchandisers who are personable, presentable, and can play well." They are also looking for people who "can work with the regional reps, and can relate well with dealers and customers alike." He goes on to say they "give special consideration to those with some retail experience and who know what not to say, as well as what to say. We don't want people who like to discuss pricing, the competition, and their own playing ability. We also don't want musicians whose egos are out of control."

Almost every major musical instrument manufacturer uses product specialists; maybe not the reed or accessory people, but definitely the horn, drum, guitar, and keyboard guys. Roland also uses recording engineers/clinicians who can demo and explain the newest recording gear. If you've got some computer smarts, know Excel, can do PPS presentations, have the ability to travel, and know a specific instrument inside out, there are jobs for you.

National music stores such as American Music Group, Music & Art Centers, Sam Ash Music, and Brook Mays Music, are also looking for talent in different areas of the country. Check their Web sites, talk to your local music dealer, or try to get a NAMM directory.

When you contact these people, even a local music dealer, be specific as to what type of work you are looking for. If you only want to teach, let that be known. If you have a talent for band instrument repair, let them know how much time you will have available. If sales are your interest or strength, let them know about your demo skills.

The most important thing to remember is that these companies want musicians who sound mature, can think on their feet, and are dependable. If you are really looking for a solid rock gig where playing clubs and concerts for days on end is your goal, then this probably won't blend with what you are trying to achieve. But if you teach, do studio work, play casual dates, and know your axe, this gig could fit in perfectly. The work is there, and the money is there too. Your office space will probably be an aisle seat on one of the major airlines. Travel is part of the gig. And these gigs could lead to something better down the road. Check it out.

Companies want to hire musicians who are mature and dependable.

Taking the Bad
with the Better

The more people who hear you play, the better your chances of getting more work. Maybe not better work, but certainly more work. The problem though, is that we are professional musicians, and sometimes we don't like the gigs we get. We tend to be selective. How many times have you thought about how much you hate playing the tunes required for a particular gig? We've all been there.

If you take just the gigs that let you play only the stuff you like, you might find yourself on public assistance by the end of the month.

If you want a lot of work, you have to play a lot of venues. There are a lot of great, broke musicians out there who are sitting at home, waiting for the right cool gigs to come along. If you want to get the work, people have to know you're out there and that you're a pro. And that means taking the good with the bad.

I know a drummer who won't do any ethnic gigs—no Polish or Yiddish affairs. He hates the stuff he has to play. And I know of a keyboard player who refuses to back up any singers who aren't worthy of his talent, not up to his caliber. These musicians do a lot of other part-time work though—driving cabs, working factory assembly lines—not to mention visiting the unemployment office.

There is a lot of work out there for musicians, if you want it. If you want to take your career to the next level, those bad jobs (at least bad in your mind) could give you the exposure you need. I know a trumpet player who does nothing else beyond playing for a living. He doesn't care where the work is. He fills in with the local symphony, he's the trumpet player people hear at the beginning of each horse race at the local track (he has to dress up for that one, too), and he plays in a Dixieland group on weekends. He also plays a few Saturday weddings with a polka band from time to time. The better gigs come too, but he turns down very few of the less-than-hip gigs. He says, "The more people who hear you, the more jobs you'll get. They may not be to your liking, but how bad do you want to work? If you're good, people will know it no matter what or where you are playing."

In the video *How to Get Gigs that Pay Big Bucks* (Hal Leonard, 2003), Richie Sambora, guitarist for Bon Jovi, said that when he was starting out he'd "play a pay toilet with his own change." Another musician on the video said, "To hone your craft, you need to be able to play anything, and play it well." You have to look as if you like it too.

Aha. There's the catch. You might hate it, but you have to play it well, and play as if you like it. A great musician with a bad attitude is worse than a fair musician with great people skills. We are in a fun business. When we play, we make people happy. Those people we make happy pay us money. At least look happy while you're working the gig. You can turn off the happy face when you get home.

You might hate it, but you have to play well— and play as if you like it.

Those people who ask for the dumb requests, who have too much to drink, who tell you they can play better than you, are sometimes the people who will be instrumental in getting you more gigs. That's because they have friends and they like to talk. So make an art out of smiling when you'd rather slap somebody. Never mind that it's the third time you've played "Shout!" or they want to hear the Macarena thing again.

One of my friends recently played a gig at a local nursing home. He told me he really didn't want to do it, but felt he owed it to the other musicians (if he didn't play, they weren't doing it either). They played for an hour in front of "very senior" senior citizens. Some of the audience didn't even know what was going on.

One person did, though. It was the daughter of one of the residents who was there visiting. She liked the group, appreciated that they drove twenty miles to come there, and hired them for a corporate venue at her company. She was the meeting planner, and that corporate show they contracted paid huge bucks.

Getting exposure will get you more work, but if you take less-than-desirable work, be professional about it. Don't whine, complain, sneer, or talk it down. You're only as good as your last gig.

CLOSING

CLOSING

Music Is an Art—To Make Money at It Is a Business

Probably not a week goes by when someone doesn't remind me about how great things were "in the old days." Bands were constantly working, clubs of all sizes were booking musicians, gigs were available for any musician who could play well. Nobody played for free, live music was everywhere, and there weren't enough musicians to go around.

Well, I don't want to burst anyone's bubble, but there really never was a time when the phone just rang off the hook, with people looking for a single, combo, or band of any size. It didn't happen. And it's not going to happen now.

If you want to work as a professional musician, you need to treat it like a business. That means networking, promo kits, demo CDs, your own PR program, business cards, brochures, voice mail (or a decent answering machine), e-mail, a Web site, and a business plan.

You also need a good attitude. A business attitude. You can't blame things you can't control for not getting yourself booked. By human nature, when things start to go wrong we like to come up with excuses. Excuses like: "The economy is bad," "Clubs want musicians to work for the door," "Mobile DJs are putting musicians out of work," or "Nobody wants to hire live musicians anymore."

On top of that, we blame the economy, the President, the town where we live, the competition, or the customers themselves. However, all things taken into consideration, it is easier to just look in the mirror and see who is actually responsible for getting work, or the lack thereof.

It's you. You are the prophet of your own destiny. To make it in the music business today, you need to let people know who you are as a musician. You need to hone your craft, and you need to tweak your business skills as well. That means marketing, selling, publicizing, networking, and promoting as well as performing. Any roadblocks you meet getting work as a musician can be overcome. It won't be easy, it will take some work, and that overnight success you're trying to achieve may take a just a little longer than overnight.

What are your goals as a professional musician? Do you have any? It could be working one of the Las Vegas casinos, backing up a famous singer, playing six nights a week at a major club, appearing on Letterman or "The Tonight Show," or simply filling your calendar in your own hometown. If you really want to make it as a musician, and if gigs are really important to you, why don't you just bite the bullet, come up with a plan, and start putting in the time, money, and effort you need to be a success? Start today.

A journey of a thousand miles begins with the first step. What are you doing right now to reach your goal? Your personal success as a professional musician is directly related to your belief in yourself and your music. Your success is in your own hands. Henry Ford said, "Whether you think you can or think you can't, you're absolutely right."

What are you doing right now to reach your goal?

So, what's your answer? Do you want to come up with a plan and give it your best shot, or do you want to just sit back in your chair, hoping things will get better, and maybe the phone will ring?

It's your choice. There are plenty of gigs out there. You need to be creative. And you need to go after them.